When Night Becomes As Day

248.8   3632

George

When night becomes day.

DATE DUE

248.8		3632
CLASS		ACC
George.		
(LAST NAME OF AUTHOR)		
When night becomes day.		
(BOOK TITLE)		

DATE DUE	ISSUED TO

First Baptist Church Library
Tomball, Texas

When Night Becomes As Day

PERSONAL STORIES OF FAITH

FOREWORD BY WAYNE E. OATES

Denise George, Compiler

BROADMAN PRESS
Nashville, Tennessee

© Copyright 1986 • Broadman Press
All rights reserved
4254-34
ISBN: 0-8054-5434-9

Dewey Decimal Classification: 248.843
Subject Headings: CHRISTIAN LIFE // WOMEN
Library of Congress Catalog Card Number: 86-6887
Printed in the United States of America

Unless otherwise noted, all Scripture quotations are taken from the King James Version of the Bible.
All Scripture quotations marked RSV are taken from the Revised Standard Version of the Bible, copyrighted 1946, 1952, © 1971, 1973.
All Scripture quotations marked NIV are taken from the HOLY BIBLE *New International Version,* copyright © 1978, New York Bible Society. Used by permission.
All Scripture quotations marked TLB are taken from *The Living Bible.* Copyright © Tyndale House Publishers, Wheaton, Illinois, 1971. Used by permission.
All Scripture quotations marked NASB are taken from the *New American Standard Bible.* Copyright © The Lockman Foundation, 1960, 1962, 1963, 1968, 1971, 1972, 1973, 1975, 1977 Used by permission

Library of Congress Cataloging-in-Publication Data

When night becomes as day.

1 Women—Conduct of life   I George, Denise
BJ1610.W53 1986   248.8'43   86-6887
ISBN 0-8054-5434-9 (pbk.)

For my cousin
Alan Leon Schrader
whose faith and courage
give me strength.

Acknowledgments

I am grateful to Dr. Wayne E. Oates, my professor and my friend, who has been a continuing encouragement to me in my writing ministry, and who, through his "Pastoral Care in Human Crisis" class at The Southern Baptist Theological Seminary, gave me the idea for this book.

To Helen Parker and Terry Helwig, for their good friendship, and for their invaluable suggestions for and help with this book, I offer a special "thank you."

To all the women who have written their stories, who have shared so freely and so intimately their struggles and victories, my deepest gratitude.

As always, I am indebted to my husband, Timothy, for his understanding support. And for my children, Christian and Alyce, who tolerate a writer-mommy, and who keep my life busy and exciting, I give my love and thanksgiving.

Contents

Foreword—**Dr. Wayne Oates**   11

Opening—**Denise George**   13

1. **Sue Monk Kidd** shares the story of a troubled Thanksgiving Day with her family.   17

2. **Judith S. Ross** tells of her life with her mother.   25

3. **Phyllis R. Pleasants** relates a difficult career decision.   33

4. **Diane Mabrey** relives the period after her thirteen-year-old son died.   47

5. **Virginia Rose "Ginger" Greene** doesn't see herself as handicapped.   59

6. **Jenny Abrams** shares how she came to forgive "the other woman."   67

7. **June Holland McEwen** has come to an understanding of her aging mother.   75

8. **Averil Peters,** normally a joyous person, moved across a state with her family and wondered why she had seemed to lose part of her joy.   81

9. **Fran Jones Snyder** remembers her life with her husband, a drug addict.   91

10. **Janet Sprouse** tells of her struggles with fear and depression.   97

11. **Judy Hamilton** shares her experience with breast cancer in the hope that it will help someone else.   107

12. **Elizabeth Puckett** relates why "the empty nest" was a problem in her home.   115

13. **Linda Hardesty** relives her days as a battered wife and how she sought help.   125

14. **Susan Coppock** feared she was having a breakdown until she realized God was showing her her wasted potential.   135

15. **Denise George** remembers where her comfort came from when she lost her grandmother.   139

16. **Helen Parker** shares her disappointment when her career choice of teaching was closed to her because of her blindness.   143

17. **Lorraine Kaufman** tells how she and her children survived the murder of her husband.   149

18. **Kathy Fogg Berry** relates how God led in hard decisions about career and family.   159

19. **Terry Helwig** felt betrayed when her father committed suicide.   165

20. **Jo Edlin** felt her faith diminish when she was led to pray for a miraculous healing, then no healing occurred.   **169**

21. **Sue Schrader** tells the story of her husband's brain surgery.   **175**

22. **Pamela Hadaway** shares how the Lord worked through her desire to adopt a baby, even when tragedy struck the child first assigned to her.   **181**

   Closing—**Denise George**   **191**

Foreword

You are about to read a unique book that records "firsthand encounters" with God. When Jesus spoke with the woman at the well, she found redemption in her personal discovery of him as the Christ her Lord. Then she went to the persons in the Samaritan village who in turn went to see Jesus the Christ for themselves. They returned to her and said: "Now we believe, not because you told us only, but because we have seen him ourselves and know of a truth that he is indeed the Christ." Their "hearsay" faith had become a firsthand encounter with Christ.

The persons in this book whom Denise George has interviewed and whose stories she presents are persons who have met, faced, and gone through severe crises. Agonizing career decisions, abandonment by a husband for another woman, struggling with depression and fear, losing a husband to drug addiction, the discovery that magical healing often does not in fact happen, the anguish over adopting a child, brutal abuse by a spouse, the multiple kinds of losses—the loss of one's sight, the loss of cherished persons by death, particularly the loss of parent by suicide —all these and more fill these pages.

Denise George chose in writing this book to consult not a large number of books but the "living human documents" of twenty-two women who had gone through severe crises. These "epistles," as the Apostle Paul wrote, are not written as books or "tablets" but as expressions of the warm tissue of hurting, broken, and healing hearts. These women faced and rose above their crises. They discovered the Presence of God, the meaning of the

Scripture in unexpected and unconventional ways. They tell their stories with realism and an amazing freedom from mouthing "easy answers" and shibboliths.

Human crises are times of testing, times of trying the human spirit. At these times we are opened up to both God and the Tempter. The Lord Jesus Christ participates in our trial with us because He Himself was tempted as we are. He becomes vividly evident to us when the going gets rough. The women who speak in these stories bear witness to His appearing.

Denise George chose to take stories of women. Consequently, this book turns out to be a "situation report" of women who are in most instances involved closely in the life of the churches. Their struggles with issues of parenthood, becoming self-determining free agents as persons, resisting the violence of men, facing the inevitability of divorce when forsaken, shakes the easy conclusion of legalistic moralists in behalf of a higher ethic of transformation through suffering.

Therefore, if you start reading this book with a halo of self-righteousness, take heed! You will be jarred by it; you will, if you persist in reading, be awed by the emergence of the Presence of God to you through these pages. You will find yourself laying down your own halo in the shadow it creates in the light of the love of Christ. You will be changed! You will know that God is no respector of persons and transcends instead of setting aside his own rules to redeem a shattered person.

I commend this book, these authors, and Denise George, the compiler, to you and am both humbled and honored to do so.

WAYNE E. OATES
Professor of Psychiatry and Behavioral Science
Director, Program in Ethics and Pastoral
  Counseling
University of Louisville School of Medicine
Senior Professor, Psychology of Religion
The Southern Baptist Theological Seminary

Opening

This is a book about women, written by women. The idea for this book came to me early one morning as I sat in Dr. Wayne E. Oates' class on Crisis Counseling at The Southern Baptist Theological Seminary in Louisville, Kentucky.

Only a month before the class began, I, myself, had struggled with a crisis—the death of my grandmother. And I knew many other Christians, both men and women, who were trying to cope with personal hardships. Throughout the semester, as I read, researched, and wrote papers, I pondered deeply the problem and pain of personal crisis. Did the event usually weaken its victim or did it make the person stronger? Indeed, the death of my grandmother, while certainly heartbreaking, had brought me nearer to God as it had caused me to pray harder for understanding and to examine my faith more deeply. This had also seemed true for many of my Christian friends who had experienced crises. Toward the end of the course, I set out to discover some answers to these questions.

In talking with others, I discovered very few Christians who had not undergone some kind of physical, emotional, or spiritual upheaval in their lives. I asked them about their crisis and about their struggle with it. How intense was their pain? How did they manage to cope from day to day? Where did they find the courage and strength to "keep on keeping on"? At what point, and why, did they pull themselves to their feet and once again get on with their lives? And, finally, as they reflected back on the experience, what had they learned from it, and how had it affected their faith in God?

These were intimate questions. They involved the sharing of one's personal, family, and spiritual life. While some backed away from my probing, many more talked openly and honestly about their struggles, as well as their discoveries about themselves, others, and God.

In thinking about putting this information together in a book, I knew I could not include all I had researched. So I narrowed the scope somewhat. While I had talked with many men who had dealt with various crises, I decided to limit the book just to women. I also realized that in the space of about two hundred pages, I could not even hope to touch on every crisis a woman might experience. So I carefully chose and invited women to write who had coped with problems—universal-type problems—ones that other women might one day have to cope with.

These are ordinary women like you and me. Many are wives and mothers. Some are single. Some work inside the home, and some work outside the home. I met and talked with many of them in various places, including Kentucky, Massachusetts, West Virginia, Tennessee, North Carolina, South Carolina, and even as far away as Switzerland (my home for one year during the assembling of this book).

Some of the women are professional writers and published authors. Many more have never written anything for publication before. All have used their own names. The women represent many different denominations of faith, and they come from various parts of the United States as well as the world. They range in age from middle twenties to early seventies. They have varied cultural, economic, and educational backgrounds. I knew some of them before I invited them to write. Many more I did not know. Most have never met each other.

In many ways, these women are very different from one another, yet, in some ways, they are alike. Each one has known intense struggle, despair, and grief. Each professes faith in and love for

Jesus Christ and, in the darkest hour of her crisis, has reached out to Him for help. And each one, in her own time and in her own way, has found the Lord's comforting Presence, has discovered a deeper faith and trust, and, as a result, has gained inner healing, courage, and victory over her crisis.

Why bring these stories together in a book? One of my favorite authors, C. S. Lewis, once wrote to his friend, Malcolm: "I think it is only in a shared darkness that you and I can really meet at present; shared with one another and, what matters most, with our Master. We are not on an untrodden path. Rather, on the main-road."[1] In their intimate and open sharing, the writers all echoed one main appeal: "I just hope my story will help and encourage someone else."

In *When Night Becomes As Day*, the aim is to show you, the reader, that you are not alone in the midst of your own personal struggle. Indeed, you are not on an "untrodden path." You are walking right down the middle of the "main-road." These women have experienced and have dealt with the same human problems that confront you and me. They could have so easily lost hope, but they didn't. Instead, in their pain, they turned to their loved ones for help—a "shared darkness"—and, most importantly, to the Loving One for hope. In doing so, they found that their darkness of night was replaced by the early morning light of day, perhaps faint at first, but brilliant by noonday.

Here are their stories. . . .

> Denise George
> Ruschlikon, Switzerland
> Fall 1985

Note

1. C S Lewis, *Letters to Malcolm, Chiefly on Prayer* (London· Fontana Books, 1963)

When morning gilds the skies, My heart awaking cries,
May Jesus Christ be praised! Alike at work and prayer,
To Jesus I repair; May Jesus Christ be praised.

The night becomes as day, When from the heart we say,
May Jesus Christ be praised! The pow'rs of darkness fear,
When this sweet song they hear, May Jesus Christ be praised.

Ye nations of mankind, In this your concord find:
May Jesus Christ be praised! Let all the earth around
Ring joyous with the sound: May Jesus Christ be praised.

In heav'n's eternal bliss, The loveliest strain is this,
May Jesus Christ be praised! Let earth, and sea, and sky
From depth to height reply, May Jesus Christ be praised.
Amen.

—Katholiches Gesangbuch, 1828

1
Hidden Blessings
by SUE MONK KIDD

Despite the tension of the last few months, we were going to have a quiet Thanksgiving day. We had found a little log cabin in the woods where we could hear pine branches brush the roof and wind sweep the mountains in the distance. It wasn't like us to be in a strange place on Thanksgiving. But somehow it had seemed important to come.

I put the turkey into the ancient-looking stove and turned to gaze at my family. My husband, Sandy, tended a fire in the fireplace, while our two children played before it on a braided rug. The scene looked so perfect . . . so content. Maybe today we could forget the problem that had consumed us for so many weeks.

"Daddy, sing Old Mac Farmer," cried five-year-old Bob. And suddenly the uneasiness was back.

A small shadow of pain moved over my husband's face. How do you explain to a child that you can't sing with him . . . that you may never sing again because you've lost your voice? Old Mac Farmer, or more correctly, "Old Macdonald Had a Farm," was their special song. My husband and son sang it with great relish and mischief, including animals in the song that poor Old MacDonald would never have wanted. Dinosaurs, warthogs, skunks and whales. I remembered the time Sandy sang, "On his farm he had a crab. Eee-i-eee-i O. With a pinch, pinch here and a pinch, pinch there. Here a pinch. There a pinch . . ." Bob had dissolved into laughter as his daddy chased him through the house, pinching lightly.

"I can't sing," Sandy struggled to explain, pushing the words out with strain and effort. His voice was barely audible in the sudden stillness of the room. A raspy whisper. He sadly gathered Bob in his arms and gazed at the flames licking up the chimney.

I turned toward the window. Beyond, the brown and bony woods of autumn drew a curtain around our little cabin.

Sandy, a campus minister and college religion teacher, had lost his voice after chest surgery. Up till then he'd had a deep, slow Georgia drawl that was rich and charming. In fact, after hearing his voice on the phone for the first time—before I ever saw him in person—I turned to my college roommate and laughingly said, "I think I'm in love." He had that kind of voice. Standing there by the cabin window, I could hear his old, self-confident voice preaching from the pulpit at First Baptist Church in Augusta, Georgia, where he began his career as a young minister. I could see him shouting at football games and calling the children in for supper from the backyard. But now all of that was gone.

He had awakened after the surgery, whispering. At first we thought it was a terrible case of laryngitis. But weeks passed and we learned that the nerve to his vocal cord had been damaged . . . paralyzed. Maybe it was temporary; perhaps it was permanent. No one seemed to know.

I could still see the look on his face the day the news came. He had clutched my hand tightly, as if he were losing his hold on everything he had worked for, everything he loved. On the campus where he ministered he had used his voice for everything: counseling, teaching, chapel services. He had worked with his voice the way a carpenter works with his hands.

"Could I be like this the rest of my life?" he whispered to the doctor. His face was incredulous.

"Wait four months and return. Then I can tell you something definite," the specialist replied.

The waiting had been worse than I'd thought. Memories drifted through my head of simple ordinary activities that had become impossible. Sandy could not be heard on the phone and had to whisper his words to me, which I relayed to the caller. He couldn't be heard by the bank teller or the gas-station attendant or the man who stopped him on the street for directions. Some people quit trying to converse with him at all; others talked to me as if he weren't even there. "Tell Sandy we hope his voice returns," a lady said while he stood right beside me.

He had managed to conduct his classes and chapel services with a portable microphone, straining his throat so much we would spend our evenings in silence. How I had missed talking with him! And in a crowd, at a ball game or a church social, he had been lost. I watched him withdraw into a little box of silence. One day when I found him staring at a ringing telephone, I went to the bedroom and cried.

At last the waiting was almost over. Sandy's appointment was the week after Thanksgiving. I suppose that's why we'd come here to the little cabin . . . to find some reprieve from the tension, some vaguely sought help.

But here we were, doubt and gloom creeping over the old cedar walls. "Please God," I thought, "help us cope." For some reason I didn't ask God to restore Sandy's voice. That prayer was nearly worn out, tattered like a kite that has flown a storm. For the first time it seemed more important to cope with the moment than with what might come.

I closed my eyes against all the memories, then opened them again on the woods outside. My attention was drawn to one tree in the distance. A giant, golden tree visible above the others. Winter had been slow coming and strangely the tree had kept some of its leaves. In the sunlight it almost appeared to be on fire, each leaf burning like a little tongue of flame.

I looked around at Sandy holding Bob on his lap. "Let's go for a walk," I said abruptly. Sandy nodded and I bundled up the children.

The four of us started down a worn path at the edge of the

woods. Soon we came to a small clearing and there in the middle of it was the tree I'd seen from the window. It was a grand tree. The kind with long serpentine branches that dipped close to earth. Sandy and I sat beneath it and watched the leaves flutter down, while Ann and Bob tossed them back up, making merry with autumn's confetti.

"Look, a spider web!" said Bob, who had come upon it while examining the underside of an old log. On the web was a spider. We squatted before it, watching it spin its exquisite silver house.

"I bet there're other treasures hidden here," I said. We began a kind of game. We found a blue bird feather in the leaves, which Ann stuck in her hair; a mysterious hole hidden by brush, which Bob assured us contained a rabbit. There was even a genuine arrowhead lying under a clump of rocks.

"Why, it's amazing how many little treasures are hidden right around this tree," whispered Sandy, who had been an arrowhead collector as a child.

All at once it occurred to me how happy and grateful we were all feeling. Suddenly I was seized by a peculiar idea. "Let's say our Thanksgiving blessing now. Right here under this tree," I said. Each Thanksgiving we went around the table as each of us pronounced something we were thankful for. We called it our Thanksgiving blessing. Funny, I'd almost forgotten about the blessing.

"Well, I'm thankful for finding this arrowhead," said Sandy, his voice quiet and fragile in the air.

"I'm thankful for spiders," said Bob. "And rabbits."

We turned to Ann. "My bird feather," she offered, plucking it from her hair and lifting it up.

I looked toward the top of the tree. "Today I'm thankful for this tree," I said simply.

As we walked back to the cabin and as we ate our Thanksgiving feast the spell of joy lingered. For a few minutes we had searched beneath the tree for the richness and beauty buried there . . . the same camouflaged blessings that we were usually too busy, upset or preoccupied to notice.

But the holiday soon ended and when we returned home the golden tree and the thank-yous said beneath it faded behind us like an amber dream. The reality of Sandy's vocal paralysis rushed back . . .

The day of Sandy's appointment I stayed home with the children. Sandy drove alone to the nearby city. All afternoon I prayed the new prayer I'd found by the cabin window. "Lord, help us cope with whatever may come."

At dusk I heard Sandy's key turn in the door. He didn't have to say a word. It was there on his face. His voice loss was permanent and irrevocable. I folded my arms around him, the darkness of the thing finally swallowing me up.

"What are we going to do?" I said.

"When the doctor first told me, I was ready to fall apart," he said against my ear. "Then, driving home, I began to remember last week at the cabin when we took that walk and came upon the tree. It kept coming to me that we should try looking at this event the same way we looked for those small hidden blessings beneath the tree. We should try to find something to give thanks for."

Hidden blessings. Sandy wanted to search the underside of this tragedy for something to give thanks for. I didn't think I could. But he was trying so hard.

So we sat on the sofa and began to look through the darkness of this experience, just as we searched through the shadows beneath the tree. And once more we found ourselves saying a Thanksgiving blessing.

"I'm thankful you're alive," I began a bit woodenly. "During your illness, we were't sure you would make it."

He grinned. "And I'm thankful we have each other, the children . . . and God."

"I'm thankful that we've become closer through all of this," I added, realizing for the first time how much it had bonded us together.

"I'm thankful I can still minister on campus," he said. "I've become more of a listener, and I've found I can relate to others and understand them much better when I'm not talking so much."

My eyes widened. "It has helped *me* to listen better, too."

Sandy's green eyes beamed at me. "We can be thankful for medical science, too," he continued. "The doctor tells me there's a new surgical procedure which can help me regain some of my voice. It will always be raspy and hoarse, but I'll have more volume than I do now."

"Oh, that's wonderful!" I cried.

We fell silent as our tensions and anguish drained away. I was beginning to feel light and strong, just as I'd felt during those transforming moments beneath the tree when we simply gave thanks for what was simply there.

We were coping! Thanks to God, we were coping. The Lord had revealed to us in the most delicate way that the secret to dealing with life's troubles is to look at them with grateful eyes. To search the underside for whatever blessings are hidden there. And then give thanks. That's when strength and joy flow in.

I leaned my head against Sandy's shoulder and heard a familiar tune float in the air between us. Whistling!

"I didn't know you could still whistle," I said.

"I didn't either," he replied, delighted at his discovery.

He ambled off toward Bob's room. He was whistling "Old MacDonald Had a Farm."

Sue Monk Kidd is a prolific writer and a contributing editor with *Guideposts.* She has published articles regularly in *Guideposts* and in publications such as *Reader's Digest, Home Life,* and others. Sue's first book will be soon released by *Guideposts.*

As mentioned in her story, Sue is married to Sandy, campus

minister at Anderson College, South Carolina. They have two children, Bob, 11, and Ann, 9.

Sandy did undergo surgery hoping it would heal his paralyzed vocal cords. It helped Sandy to recover some vocal strength; however, he still speaks with a bit of raspiness.

This chapter is reprinted from *Guideposts* Magazine by kind permission of the publisher.

2
My Life with Mother
by JUDITH S. ROSS

Guilt overwhelmed me; still, I hated her. *What kind of monster am I?* I wondered. *What kind of person hates her own mother?*

It was a gusty March day in the Midlands of South Carolina. Looking out Mother's hospital window, I watched the wind whisk leaves and papers off the ground, spin them round and round, then send them spiraling through the air. Like those dispirited objects, I, too, was caught in a whirlwind.

"Can't you stay with me just one night?" Mother had pleaded that afternoon before drifting off to sleep.

Those words that should have pierced me to the core only nudged my conscience and made me uneasy. Even worse, they caused my bitterness to surface as I tried to rationalize away my resentments.

"Just one night, just one night," her words echoed furiously through my mind. How I'd wished as a teenager for "just one night" to have a *real* mother—one I could talk to, share with. How many times had I come home from a date hoping, literally praying, just once she'd be in her room or at least out of sight. But as I opened the door, there she'd sit in plain view, paralyzed by alcohol, like a department-store manikin—lifeless, except for the slight bobbing of her head and tremors of her fingers and lips. Embarrassed and sorry for me, my date would quickly say goodnight.

Yet here in her hospital room more than a decade later—no

alcohol, no tremors—still—she lay so still while cancer ran rampant throughout her body.

She's my mother, I thought as I looked at her frail figure on the bed. *I want desperately to forget, to bury the painful memories of the past. But just when the old wounds begin to heal, she seems to find a way to hurt me again—alcohol always the culprit, the dividing wall.* . . .

Phil and I'd been married nine years. We wanted a baby more than anything. But before I turned twenty-five, the doctors discovered I had fibroid tumors and said I needed surgery—a complete hysterectomy. We'd hoped to get a baby through a local adoption agency. Although we'd been approved, our counselor continuously reminded us, "Babies are scarce. We can't promise you'll *ever* get a baby." After wondering, waiting for three agonizing years, we got the call.

"Congratulations, we have a beautiful eight-pound baby boy for you," our counselor said in an excited voice. Elated, I hurried over to Mother's to share our exhilarating news.

"Why couldn't you have called me on the phone? Why'd you come over here just to tell me *that?*" she asked indignantly.

In my excitement, I'd forgotten it was after 6:00 PM—her drinking time. Crushed, I left without her blessing or any indication of joy on her part about being a grandmother. . . .

As the door to her hospital room swung open, the light from the hallway flooded the hollow darkness. The aide rolled a small table over to her bed, placed the tray on it routinely, and swung it across her lap. As if oblivious to Mother sleeping, she said, "Here's your dinner. Don't you want to eat something?"

"I'll help her," I said.

"Are you her daughter?" she asked.

I smiled while nodding yes.

"I met your sister the other night. You two don't look anything alike."

"She favors Mother and I favor my daddy," I explained.

As the aide left, I uncovered the dishes. Mother shook her head. Nothing appealed. Then she pointed to the milk and coffee. As she sipped the milk, then the coffee, I could tell even swallowing was painful for her. While Mother was having dinner, my sister arrived. She'd worked all day; now she was here to stay through the night. I felt awful. But unlike Mother and me, they were close. She was Mother's favorite. She'd appeased Mother by pretending the drinking, fussing, and fighting never happened. She never mentioned it.

I'd begged, pleaded, threatened and even poured liquor down the sink in my desperation to rid our family of the problem. But not my sister. She was an enigma to me. *How had she kept it all in?* I wondered. *How had she been able to deal all these years with her pain?* Yes, we were different—now and even back then. . . .

During the hour's drive home, I thought about my sister and me when we were children—so long ago, yet only yesterday. Her hair so blonde, mine so dark. I remembered Mother saying how my sister's hair shone like yellow gold and mine like black coal in the sunlight as we played in the yard each day till dusk . . . .

Yes, dusk. When I was little, Mother always put me to bed with the sunset. As she tucked me in she'd always say, "Don't call Mama 'cause she's busy?" I'd answer in echo, "Don't call Mama 'cause she's busy."

"Night, night," she'd say as she kissed her fingertips and blew the kiss my way. I'd pretend to catch her kiss and rub it into my cheek. Then, as a rule, I'd sleep till morning.

But one night I woke up, and like any typical six-year-old, I hopped out of bed to find her. Wandering into the kitchen, I found her standing over the sink pouring a colorless liquid from a strange-looking flat bottle into a V-shaped glass. After drinking a couple times from the glass, she poured more into a regular glass and mixed it with what I recognized as ginger ale. As I stood there watching, my skinny frame hidden by the huge cabinet which towered over me, I innocently asked:

"What's that, Mama?"

Startled, she turned around abruptly. Frightened, I gasped. *That can't be my mama!* Her soft, pretty face looked harsh and ugly with her brow crinkled that way; her laughing blue eyes were now colored an angry red; and her sweet mouth was drawn and twisted.

"Uh, uh . . . it's medicine. Now go back to bed," she snapped.

Puzzled, yet mostly hurt, I crawled back into bed. Even as I drifted off to sleep, I sensed that my mother had lied to me for the first time. The next day, nothing was said about the incident, but the memory of that night lingered.

Lost in my thoughts while still driving home, I was nearly blinded by tears and the glare of lights in the rear-view mirror. I felt the need to recall a happy childhood memory . . . my eighth birthday. Mother had loved me in her own way. I remembered my cake with the white icing and pink rosebuds with green leaves. My birthstone—a real diamond ring. Just what I'd wanted. It was only a tiny diamond, but a genuine diamond ring. My sister had given me a Howdy-Doody puppet. I can still picture it—those smiling red lips and freckled cheeks. What a wonderful birthday. No little girl could have asked for a more perfect day. . . .

But there was always night. I remember I slept that night wearing my ring and holding Howdy-Doody. Suddenly I woke up—my sister shaking me:

"You gonna lie there and let them kill each other? You gonna sleep through the whole thing? Come on and help me!" As she jumped out of bed and ran toward the kitchen, I followed close behind.

There to my amazement, I saw Mama and Daddy standing in the kitchen yelling at each other. Daddy was shaking his finger in Mama's face:

"Don't you know when to quit? Don't you know when you've had enough? You're killing me. God only knows what you're doing to yourself."

Mama was trying desperately to get away from him and to her liquor in the cabinet, but Daddy, six feet and two hundred pounds, had her trapped.

Then my eleven-year-old sister began to whimper saying, "Please Daddy, don't hurt Mama." But they didn't seem to hear her. Horrified, I watched Mama try to push Daddy out of her way, but Daddy easily resisted her. Then they began to struggle. Everybody I depended on seemed to be losing control. I knew I had to do something and quick. Scurrying to the other side of the cabinet, I grabbed a big, sharp butcher knife and held it between them—the pointed end toward Daddy. "Stop it," I yelled, "or I'll use this thing." Instantly everyone was silent. Then—

"Put that knife down," Daddy said in an uncertain voice that told me he thought I might use it.

"Then promise you'll quit fussing and go to bed," I bargained. It worked. My bizarre behavior had caused them to focus their attention on me and stop fighting. But what did they think? That their eight-year-old daughter had gone mad? I didn't know; nor did I care. It had accomplished what I wanted—peace between my parents, at least until next time.

Tears streaming down my face, I was sobbing by the time I reached home. I parked the car, took a deep breath as I got out, and thought, *How will it all end?*

I must have looked pitiful as I entered the house because my precious four-year-old began to comfort me as soon as he saw me.

"Don't cry anymore, Mommie," he said in a concerned voice. I reached down, picked him up, and held him close.

"God is going to take Grandmama to heaven and give her a brand-new body," he said as he cupped both his little hands on either side of my face. "Then He's going to send her back just for you." I kissed him as I smiled through my tears. How tender, how innocent, the comfort of a little child. I had no doubt he was sent to me straight from heaven.

Later that evening, Phil asked, "What were all the tears about tonight?"

Full of cry, I said, "My mother, I'm losing her and I never had her. But tonight, as I thought about my childhood, God helped me realize I hate everything liquor did to her and our family, but I don't hate *her*. She's my mother, the only one I have. I love her though we've not been close like I'd wanted. I have to make my peace with her. Will you take me to the hospital tomorrow?"

Late the next afternoon, Phil drove me to the hospital. He waited in the car while I went in alone. It was nearly dusk. I'd brought her a beautiful peachy-colored peignoir set. She loved it. I could tell by the spark in her soft blue eyes. As she opened the package, I realized I couldn't ask her to forgive me for all the years of resentment, nor tell her I'd forgive her for the pain she'd caused me. I knew too, I couldn't ask her why—she probably didn't even know. But I knew I could tell God how I felt about her. Feeling a bit awkward I said, "I know we haven't done this together much, but could we pray?"

Cradling her in my arms, I told God what was breaking my heart:

"Dear God, thank you for my mama. I love her and I wish you would make her well so we could be close—a real mother and daughter. Be close to both of us, whatever your will for her and me. Let us feel you're near. Amen."

Although I was crying, when I lifted my head she was smiling. Stunned, I said, "Mother, you don't even have a tear."

"I don't usually cry when I'm happy," she said sweetly, reaching out to hug me.

"Oh, Mama, I love you," I said embracing her.

As I left her hospital room, I felt a deep peace as if God had reached down and touched my aching heart. Although we'd lost forever those wasted years, I knew we'd forever buried the animosities and regrets of yesterday. In our own way we'd both said, "Although I've failed you and rejected you in so many ways, I've always loved you and cared about you." Now I felt happy and free from the hate and guilt that had crippled me all those years.

As I stepped out into the night, I looked up at the nearly blackened sky. It seemed the stars were brighter than ever before. They blinked and twinkled as if rejoicing with me. The light of the full moon illuminated the sky, making the darkness seem almost like daylight. I got into the car, and Phil and I rode hand in hand toward home.

Judith S. Ross is a free-lance writer living in Orangeburg, South Carolina with her husband and ten-year-old son. She teaches English and creative writing. She has been published in *Home Life* Magazine and *Marriage and Family Living*. She holds a B.A. from the University of South Carolina in English and has completed some graduate work toward her M.A. in English with special emphasis in creative writing. She is a member of the First Presbyterian Church, where she is involved in an evangelistic ministry. She received an Inspirational Award at the 1985 Anderson Writer's Conference.

3
My Difficult Career Decision

by PHYLLIS R. PLEASANTS

The chapel speaker was talking about prayer as the gateway to experiencing God's grace, when he cited another source as saying: "The big question about prayer is not 'Did you get what you asked for?' but, rather, 'When you have struggled through and wrestled with God like Jacob, did you yield? Did you allow yourself to become surrendered and obedient to the will of God?'"

Did you yield? That question ricocheted around my brain. *If that's the definition of prayer, then I guess my whole life was a prayer for the three years it took me to get here,* I thought. *But why doesn't anyone ever point out that yielding is not a one-time-for-all-time thing? The real question is not "Did you yield?" once, but "Did you yield?" again and again every time the issue surfaced.*

After chapel I continued to reflect on how much the issue of yielding had been a part of my life during the three years that passed between my asking God's help with my career struggle and my arrival at seminary. It had all seemed so easy and straightforward in the beginning. Feeling as if I were drowning in frustration with my job, I turned to the Lord. It was a reluctant turning, even an angry one because this was one area I was trying to make it "on my own." Even though I was a committed Christian, there were still areas in which I needed to grow. My career search was one of them. It was one area of my life where I had not put the Lord first over my wants and desires and others' expectations and standards of success. Reading Isaiah 6:8 one morning in the spring of 1981, I finally reached the point where I could say willingly and sincerely, "Here am I, Lord. Send me." Use me. Guide me. And I thought that was it. I was finally ready to let God lead me in a career choice rather than me telling God what I was going to do and asking God to bless it. I have to smile now as I remember how confident I was then that I had yielded to God. I thought that was all there was to it.

I even told my husband, Conrad, about my decision to let the Lord lead me, and he was encouraging. Neither of us had any idea what was in store for us. Seminary never entered either of our minds. At this time we had been married three years after a rocky six-year courtship. I met Conrad, twenty-nine years older than I am, while I was in graduate school in the city where he was a career police officer. Our age, education, and cultural differences contributed a lot to our drawn-out courtship. However, we have felt for almost thirteen years now that we are a gift of God to each other. When I told Conrad I had yielded my career frustration and search to the Lord, that was fine with him. He even offered to pray for me that there would be a resolution to my struggle. It seemed so easy.

Conrad had retired shortly after we married, and at this time we were living in the Washington, D.C. area where I was a legislative and research assistant for a small housing finance trade association. Later I became a lobbyist for that same organization. I worked two blocks from the White House and regularly came into contact with staffers from both House and Senate Banking committees on legislation. We had a house in northern Virginia, and we belonged to a wonderful church. We were beginning to "make it," I suppose, in the eyes of some people, when I was overwhelmed with discontent. Even though a million women may have gladly traded places with me, I was very unhappy in my job and felt I was headed nowhere on a treadmill called life. I just knew there had to be more than this. I couldn't believe God created life to be a treadmill, so I began searching for what I could do to change me and my attitude.

That fall, while Conrad was on his annual hunting expedition, yielding became a part of my faith pilgrimage again. I really can't describe what happened. All I know is that during the silence and solitude of having the house to myself for the week, I encountered the Lord and became convinced I was being called to full-time ministry—to do on a full-time scale what I had done voluntarily for years, particularly through the Christian education programs of the church I belonged to. At first I was scared to admit it. Then I wanted to sing and shout. "Of course! No wonder I am so miserable—I am in the wrong area. I've been denying my gifts and trying to be something I'm not. I've been trying to meet the world's standard of success, not my own, and certainly not God's." Then I decided, "No, this can't be. (Some people will think of anything when they want out of a situation badly enough.) That would just be leaving a situation that is difficult in order to run to a situation that is comfortable. After all, I am a preacher's daughter, have been around churches all my life. That's not God speaking; that's desperation."

After two friends out of the blue said they thought I would be happier doing church work for a career than lobbying, I decided I'd better pay attention. Maybe God was calling me after all instead of my being desperate to leave my job. In spite of my fears of Conrad's reaction, I decided to tell him what had happened as soon as he came home.

Conrad is a great person to test spiritual events on because he is a realist. If something can't be seen, tasted, touched, heard, or smelled, it's not real. At this point, spiritual concepts were not part of Conrad's frame of reference. Not that he was an unbeliever. He just didn't have many unexplainable things in his life, except maybe me. But I didn't really think about all that. I only knew that Conrad never felt compelled to tell me what I wanted to hear, and I trusted that gift. I knew if my being in full-time ministry was totally unreasonable, and made no sense given who I am as a person, Conrad would be the first to tell me.

Needless to say, Conrad was startled by my latest experience.

However, he finally said, "Well, I want you to be happy. Let's see what happens. Go ahead, test it, and see what you find out." Once again I had yielded, and it had seemed so easy. I was beginning to wonder why I had been so stubborn about not yielding to God completely before.

My initial inquiries quickly revealed to me that I was going to have to go back to school. I had hoped to be able to make a career switch with the educational credentials I already had, but more and more, seminary loomed as an inevitable requirement. I wrote to several seminaries requesting information about their degree programs. As the information came in from the seminaries, and I began receiving answers to my inquiries that indicated seminary was necessary, Conrad began to withdraw his support. I denied it at first, since he never said anything, but I could sense the tension every time he got the mail and there was something in it for me related to my search. I couldn't understand this because I thought his support was the one certain thing in my life right now. Finally, I couldn't stand it anymore, and one night as we were getting ready for bed I decided to try to get him to talk about the situation. After a few probing questions from me, he decided to let me have it:

"Called? I don't know what you mean by called! No one's spoken to me. I'm telling you God, Himself, is going to have to come here and talk to me personally if we're supposed to sell everything, move, and start over. I met you, remember? the last time you were in school. And I can tell you one thing: I did not retire to live in *that* poverty! Don't tell me we can make it on my retirement! I know we can't. Now, just forget the whole thing! Grow up, and learn to be happy with what you have. Your job wouldn't be so miserable if you would put as much energy into your work as you do trying to get away from there!"

With that outburst, my heart almost stopped. How could he talk like that?! Where was my ever supportive, wise, understanding, encouraging husband? I was devastated. Why couldn't he understand how important this was to me? Why hadn't he said anything before? What had been going on in him for the past year while I had been exploring and searching? I thought he was with me. Now this. After what seemed like hours, but was really only minutes, I managed to respond, "I feel certain God is leading me in the direction of full-time ministry. I'm not sure what all that means, except it is becoming more obvious it will mean going to school again. I am confident of one thing—God is not leading me to get a divorce. If God is truly leading me then he will lead you, too."

I couldn't believe it. With those words I had committed myself to waiting for God's leadership in all aspects of my life, and waiting for things to happen on God's time, not my own. That was not my usual pattern. Here I was after searching for a year, ready to apply to seminary and, when accepted, to put our house on the market, quit my job, and move. I had been busy, busy, busy. Too busy trying to make things happen to wait on the Lord.

But now the most important person in my life seemed unalterably opposed to my deepening commitment. The intensity of Conrad's outburst made me feel I had two choices: begin cajoling, begging, and trying to guilt him into supporting my decision to return to school, or continue loving him and try to understand his opposition while waiting for the Lord to work with Conrad. After realizing that manipulating Conrad could have disastrous consequences for our marriage and my future ministry, I decided to wait upon the Lord. It was one of the hardest, scariest decisions of my life. I thought I had committed all my life a year ago, that I had yielded fully to God. That was only the beginning. Learning to wait was another part of my yielding, and perhaps harder for me than yielding to God's call in the first place.

By choosing to wait upon the Lord I was choosing to let Conrad decide for himself. I was choosing to let Conrad work out his relationship with the Lord. What if he didn't respond? What would I do? Would there ever be a situation where the Lord would lead me that would be without Conrad? I couldn't even imagine that happening, except in case of death. Maybe that was it. Maybe I was being led to prepare myself to do something after he was dead. That's awful! I couldn't think I would have to be patient that long. The alternative—that he might die soon—was so horrible I shuddered the moment the thought crossed my mind.

While sharing with my father my disappointment in Conrad's reaction, I received another blow. He agreed with Conrad! What was going on here? The more I thought I was yielding to God, the more topsy-turvy my world seemed to become. My father was a dedicated preacher and denominational leader in the state. He had been my pastor for the first eighteen years of my life, and I had grown up witnessing his *deep* commitment to the Lord regardless of the cost. For example, he had taken a significant cut in pay to do what he felt God was leading *him* to do the year I went off to college. Poor timing for a pay cut, wouldn't you think? How could he advise me not to pursue what *I* thought was God's leadership in *my* life?

It was so unbelievable. My mother and my brother, with whom I couldn't agree on anything when I was growing up (not even whether or not the sun was shining), were very supportive of me in this situation. In fact, I almost missed their support and almost didn't recognize it because I was so sure my support would come from where it had always come—my husband and my father. And they were the two most adamantly opposed!

I was plunged into doubt and questioning. What about all those stories I had heard all my life about people finally deciding to follow God rather than trying to lead Him around by the nose? Everything seemed to work for them. Peace, happiness, support. Where was that for me? And I was getting such mixed messages from my pastor, another significant person during this period. "It's obvious God is leading you"; "You have many talents"; "Don't go to seminary, you have enough education and experience already"; "Look for something here"; "Maybe God is leading you, but not away from here where you already have a significant ministry with our youth"; "Whenever God closes a door, He always opens a window." I almost gagged when I heard that. I wasn't ready for that right now. I was so surprised at the door being closed after just a glimpse of hope that I couldn't see any windows!

Deep reflection on what was happening led me to understand Conrad and my father better. Daddy was being Daddy. When he could be Phil, he was thrilled with my determination for deeper commitment, and he applauded my decision to follow God's leadership—whatever the cost. But when he was Daddy, he was very afraid, and he wanted to protect his daughter. He wanted me safe, secure, happy, and financially well off, rather than having to struggle because of a commitment. Mostly, he felt compelled to test me, to be brutally realistic about the cost of commitment, knowing he couldn't live with himself if he painted a rosy picture and my decision turned out to be a disastrous mistake. He knew God's leadership in his own life, but no one can know that for someone else, and he was afraid for me.

Conrad had very specific reasons for not being able to accept what I considered the miracle in my life. For one thing, Conrad loves me very much, and he knew how miserable I was in my job. He was afraid I was running away and trying to use God to make it more acceptable. His fear was not groundless. I had considered that possibility, too. This situation was different, but only time could convince him of that.

And there was the issue of money. The one major area in our lives where you could tell there was twenty-nine years difference in our ages was in the area of finances. Conrad came to maturity during the Depression, when his family lost everything, including his parents. That fear of financial insecurity could not be erased, even after thirty-seven years in a successful career which was financially stable even if not very lucrative. I frequently forgot about his financial anxieties, though, because I came to maturity in the sixties, when it seemed life would always just get better and better. I believed in credit and a healthy use of inflation to make life better. Conrad had apoplexy over the amount of debt we had on our house, and he never could see the tax advantages to using credit. I had convinced him buying this house would be a good thing, and now I was trying to talk him into moving.

Moving was another issue. Conrad had never lived anywhere other than the area where he was born and raised, until he married me. He moved from there to northern Virginia, first to an apartment and then to a house, and now I was talking about moving again—to another state. And this had all occurred in four years of marriage! The more I thought about the situation, the more amazed I was that I had assumed Conrad would support me in the first place. We were beginning to get established financially. We had a house we loved in a community we enjoyed, and we were active in a church that was leading both of us to grow in our faith. Conrad couldn't believe God would lead us away from all of this. I was beginning to feel deeply chagrined at how easy I thought yielding was, and how shallow I had been to accept Conrad's initial offers of support at face value. I thought I had already wrestled with God, but that had only been the preliminaries.

After much questioning and reflecting, I began to feel maybe my pastor was right. God was leading me to deeper commitment, but right here where I was. Nothing dramatic, but to stay put. That was harder for me. I wanted to make a glorious sacrifice, do something dramatic to prove my commitment. But what was my response to which I kept returning throughout this process? "Here am I, Lord. Send me." And maybe that's what God was doing—sending me to more extensive involvement in ministry right where I was. After prayer I realized that if I was as committed as I claimed to be, I had to be committed to that possibility as well.

Conrad and I became even more involved with the teenagers in our church. Both of us experienced God's presence in our lives through those young people. They ministered to us as much as we ministered to them. There was truly a family feeling—for us and about thirty teenagers. It was wonderful! But I didn't stop looking for more to do.

Then a church in the D.C. area expressed an interest in me for a staff vacancy they had. The pastor was willing to work with someone who had experience regardless of degree credentials, and he was very encouraging to me when I met with him. He was excited about my years of volunteer experience, and he felt my years of experience in the political world of D.C. more than outweighed my lack of seminary education as far as meeting the ministry needs of his church. The person vacating the job had recommended me, and everything seemed to be going very positively.

In the middle of the interview process with that church I discovered I needed surgery for a tumor. That was a frightening experience for me and Conrad, but he was very steadfast. Conrad cared for me beautifully, and both of us allowed ourselves to hope that, upon my recovery, I would have a new job. Conrad was more supportive of my attempt to find a ministry position in the D.C. area where we would not have to uproot and begin again. He really was the encouraging, supportive husband I had come to depend on, not the husband of the outburst a year earlier.

While I was recuperating at home from the surgery, I received the news that the church, while very impressed with me, had decided to hire someone with a seminary degree. Before I could fully absorb that blow, my church gave me another position of ministry to which I felt called. Although it was not a staff position, this was the most meaningful thing to ever happen to me. And, I thought, this is it. This is the commitment I was being led to make. I thought I was yielding again to God's leadership, and I entered into this ministry enthusiastically. There was still something tugging at me, but so much had happened, I couldn't recognize it at the time.

As we were leaving on vacation that summer, we received the worst news of our entire marriage. My hospitalization insurance refused to pay for my surgery of three months before, and I was partially, unknowingly responsible. I had relied on bad advice without investigating the situation myself, and now the worst had happened. The summer of 1983 was the worst summer of my life as I alternated between shock, anger, despair, depression, guilt, and looking for God in all this. While we may have had a stable financial situation, we weren't at all sure it could handle this blow. What in the world was going on? Two years earlier I committed my life to full-time ministry and following God's leadership. Since then it seemed there was just escalating disappointment, frustration, and closed doors. "God, where are you in all this?" I screamed.

In the midst of my despair one day, Conrad said, "Maybe going to seminary is what you should do. I thought you shouldn't go because of giving up financial security, but this whole situation has shown me there isn't such a thing as financial security. And our Christian friends at church are the ones who have supported us and stood by us through all of this, not the people you work for. You're good at what you do, especially with the kids. Maybe you should go." The people in our church, including the teenagers, had been wonderful, and they had allowed both of us to experience God in the midst of a lot of fear and pain.

That fall I had another week of vacation which we were going to use to visit my grandparents. Because they lived only an hour away from one of the seminaries I was most interested in, Conrad agreed to visit the school while we were visiting my grandparents. After we toured the campus and met with administrative personnel, we were driving to my grandparents'—in silence. I was too scared to say anything. I had been so impressed with the school, and I felt certain this was where I should be. There was such a strong feeling of pull to this place, but from previous experience, I was very reluctant to share that with Conrad. I couldn't take one more disappointment. Conrad was always quiet, but on this ride the silence was deafening. What on earth was he thinking? How did he feel about this place? The dean had been most interested in him and solicitous of him. What did

Conrad think about him? A million questions flooded my mind, and I began to fear a very long trip to my grandparents', and a very long visit where we avoided the issue between us.

Conrad broke the silence by turning to me and saying as we rode along, "I believe everyone deserves the chance to do what makes them happy. I enjoyed my career for thirty-seven years without worrying about money, ambition, or power. I received a lot of satisfaction out of knowing that I was doing something that mattered to a lot of people and that I did it well. I believe you deserve the chance to do the same, and I will do everything I can to make that possible. I like this seminary, and if everyone is like the dean, I think it will be a good place to be. You apply to the seminary when we get home, and we will see what happens from there."

I could have wept copious tears of joy, but that would have unnerved Conrad. (You're never supposed to notice when he makes a momentous decision, but just act like he was thinking this way all along.) Instead I just beamed and prayed a silent "Thank you, Lord" all the way to my grandparents'.

My testing was not over just because Conrad and I were finally united in what we felt God was leading us to do. The year between my visiting the seminary and my arriving there as a student turned out to be one of my happiest ever. Ironically, the situation at my job turned around. I began to receive the responsibility and recognition that I had worked so hard for all along. There was even the promise of a significant pay increase to accompany a promotion I received. But, even with dollars hanging in front of us, neither Conrad nor I felt we had made a mistake in committing ourselves to seminary, moving, and starting all over. We were able to handle the hospital bill situation, and money was not the motivating factor for either of us anymore. Even when the sale of our house fell through, and we were afraid we would have to move and still carry the house payment without my salary, we were not discouraged. That news would have been fatal earlier, but this time we were confident God was leading us instead of us floundering around on our own. We were thrilled when I was accepted by the seminary and received financial assistance from an independent scholarship fund.

The waiting and yielding again and again every time my commitment was challenged was not easy. However, the three years it took for both of us to wrestle with God, and to yield, now appear well worth the difficulty. Those years were years of growth for us, both individually and as a couple. They were years of strengthening and bonding of our relationship to each other and to the Lord. We received so much support from our church, and we developed deep friendships with Christian friends that never would have occurred if we had gone to seminary when I first thought we should. I received so much affirmation of my spiritual gifts from my church that I would have missed completely. My experience there has been invaluable in what I am preparing to do now.

Finally, my doubts about whether I truly was being led by God or willing to do anything to escape a bad job were put to rest. It was worth the wait to have the confidence of knowing I was leaving a job where I honestly could have stayed, but God was calling me out to a different type of service. Knowing that I was running *to* a new opportunity instead of running away from unhappiness has made all the difference in how I handled the challenges of my first year at seminary. There is nothing easy about waiting on the Lord and yielding again and again every time your commitment is challenged. However, going through the process is worth it in terms of the blessings received.

Whenever I reflect on the journey of faith I experienced in reaching this point in my life, I often remember the story in Luke of the Gadarene demoniac. When asked his name, the demoniac replied "Legion" because the devils that tormented him were many. Frequently during this pilgrimage I, too, have felt as if my name were Legion because the fears, doubts, and insecurities that tormented me were many. However, like the Gadarene demoniac, because of encounters with my Lord, I, too, can write to you today and share with you what the Lord has done for me. My relationships with both my husband and my God are stronger because of my decisions to yield my life to God's leadership, to wait for God to lead in his own way, in his own time.

Isaiah 40:31 says, "But they that wait upon the Lord shall renew their strength; they shall mount up with wings as eagles; they shall run, and not be weary; and they shall walk, and not faint." I can testify to you today that regardless of whether I am soaring, running, or walking, I feel this Scripture assures us that those who wait on the Lord move forward in their faith strengthened by the God who moves ahead of us and alongside of us on our journey. May it ever be so for you as it has been for me.

Phyllis Rodgerson Pleasants graduated with a bachelor's degree from Mary Washington College and a Master's degree from the University of Virginia. She taught school for two years and managed a law office for two more years before becoming involved in legislative work in Washington, D.C. for seven years. In 1984 Phyllis entered Southern Baptist Theological Seminary in Louisville, Kentucky, and intends to graduate with a Master of Divinity degree in 1987.

Phyllis grew up in Bon Air, a suburb of Richmond, Virginia, where her father was the founding pastor of the Bon Air Baptist Church before going to the Virginia Baptist General Board as director of the department of missions. Her mother is a reading specialist with the Chesterfield County School System. She has a younger brother, Tom, who is a pastor in Hyattsville, Maryland, and a younger sister, Ruth Ann Hess, who is a social worker in Peoria, Illinois.

Phyllis is married to Conrad N. Pleasants, who was a police officer in Charlottesville, Virginia, before retiring in 1979.

4
The Death of My Son
by DIANE MABREY

I held the yearbook in my hand. The cover boldly stated *Zenith, 1980*. I had looked forward to seeing this book, but now I hesitated. I knew that there would be pictures of young people I had come to know and love—pictures of Nathan, Renee, John, and Genie; pictures of my own boys, Rusty and Mark. Now I would be able to put faces with the names of friends and teachers at Christiansen Academy in Venezuela. These were the people I had heard my boys speak of so often when they were away at boarding school.

I opened the book and thumbed through. There were bright faces of busy children, doing the things of childhood. Then I came to the page that I knew would be there. It read: "In Memory of Mark." Mark's picture was almost a full page. He had a big smile, and he needed a haircut. His eyes were looking right at me, shining. The page read: "He couldn't hide his academic abilities, they were exceptional. He was an outstanding athlete for his age group; the coach's eyes sparkled when Mark picked up a basketball. He was a hope and a promise to all who knew him. In his one semester at C.A. people grew to love him—they couldn't help it; that's just the way Mark was. He would do anything for you, giving of himself in any way he could. Always anxious to help and encourage, diligent in every task put before him, that was Mark.

"He was born in Louisville, Kentucky, on November 17, 1966. He enrolled as a student at C.A. for the 1979-1980 school year and immediately fit into the Academy's way of life. While downhill skate-boarding on Sunday afternoon, February 10, 1980, he collided with an oncoming car and was killed. Mark Mabrey played hard and he died hard, but not for a useless cause. The suddenness of Mark's death has awakened many to the importance of making today count for Jesus Christ. We, the students and staff of Christiansen Academy, unite our hearts with fond memories. Thank you, Mark, for all you've taught us."

Once again the anger returned, but this time I immediately felt guilty. I knew that this was meant to be a tribute, but what did they mean, "He did not die for a useless cause"? He was only thirteen years old! Is this all that his life was to come to, a full-page picture and two paragraphs in a book that would soon be put on a closet shelf and forgotten? Surely not! Does tragedy have to occur before we awaken to the importance of "making today count for Jesus Christ"? Did Mark's death really mean anything to those children and teachers? Even in my anger, I knew that it had. Many of those children had watched Mark die that day.

Actually, that day started out for Russ, my husband, and me just like any other Sunday since his company had moved us to Venezuela, a year and a half ago. We had no feelings of impending doom as we drove the forty-five-minute drive down the coastal highway to church. It was a scenic panorama of white beaches and aqua blue waters. Of course, the boys weren't with us. It was difficult to have them so far away at boarding school. Christiansen Academy was an English-speaking, Christian school usually reserved only for the children of missionaries serving in South America or the Caribbean area. We had been very fortunate to have them accepted. Now, we were all looking forward to the end of the school year when it would be time for us to return to our home in Michigan and to be a family once again.

Today would be special because our friends from church had invited us to spend the afternoon with them. The men had just gone off to play tennis. Marge and I had settled ourselves on the couch when the telephone rang. I couldn't help but overhear her conversation. "Hello. Yes? Oh, how are you? That's right, John, your parents are not at home today. May I give them a message for you? Well, they are here with us. . . . What kind of an accident?"

I knew that she was talking to John Tindall. He was a "missionary kid" and a student at C.A. His father was our pastor.

Suddenly, Marge was crying, and not just crying, but sobbing. I sat very still. I could tell that something awful had happened and that it concerned us. Soon Marge was beside me on the couch. She had stopped crying. "Diane," she said, "There has been an accident and one of your boys has been hurt."

"All right, one of my boys has been hurt." I could accept that. "Just tell me that he is alive and that he will get better."

"I can't do that," she answered, "they said that Mark has been killed!"

From that moment on, my life changed. Never would it return to "normal" again. The men were summoned and told. Our overwhelming thought was that we had to go home, and, of course, it had to be a mistake.

Russ confirmed the news by calling the school and talking to the principal. I heard him asking about Rusty and charging them to take good care of him until we could get there in the morning. Then he hung up and we were alone. Never had we been so alone. I don't remember just how long we sat there, but a telephone call set in motion a series of events.

Russ's boss called. He never called on a Sunday afternoon, but he called on this Sunday afternoon. Russ said, "I'm sorry, but I won't be coming to work tomorrow. I have to see about my son." In Russ's relating the events to his boss, the reality of Mark's death began to be confirmed in our own minds.

Again, we were alone, but not for long. First one came, and then another, and another. Before long the house was filled. The men talked softly in the corner, while the women sat with me. My body was still, but my mind was active. It focused clearly on the many things that had to be done before we could leave the house and fly with Mark to the United States for his burial. It was all very logical. My mind could deal with it perfectly. Somehow we made it through the night.

The next morning, the company generously put their airplane at our disposal. They also provided us with a medical doctor and legal counsel. Two Christian friends accompanied Russ and me. Counting the two pilots, there were eight of us on the plane when it arrived at the small private airport. Rusty and members of the school's staff soon joined us.

When a Venezuelan couple entered, they were introduced as Senor and Senora Contreras. They had two children enrolled at C.A., and they stated with certainty that we would be staying in their home. Much to my surprise, the school staff encouraged us to stay in the home of these total strangers. The other five men in our party found hotel rooms, but Russ, Rusty, Beverly Tindall (John's mother), and I stayed in the Contreras home for three nights.

Senor Contreras was a medical doctor and the director of the local hospital, where Mark's body had been taken after his accident. He and his wife were Christians, and their ministry was to provide assistance and Christian hospitality to foreigners in need. We were not the first family whom they had taken into their home.

Senora Contreras made her home our headquarters. She cooked for all nine of us, sometimes three meals a day; the men made generous use of her telephone; Rusty's entire class from C.A. was received and refreshed in her living room. She didn't speak any English and my Spanish had disappeared. She did all of this with two young children in the house.

Senor Contreras led my husband through the complicated and difficult steps necessary to prepare Mark's body and have it released from the hospital and the morgue, as well as dealing with the local and state officials. Next, the body had to be put onto an airplane and taken to Caracas. Our company arranged for someone to meet Mark's body and see that it was taken first to a Venezuelan funeral home and later to the United States Embassy. All of this was necessary and had to be done properly if the body was to be allowed to leave Venezuela and to enter the United States. Normally, it takes fourteen days to accomplish everything. Mark's body was released in four days.

If the Contrerases had walked around in long white robes, complete with wings and haloes, we wouldn't have been surprised. Truly, they were ministering angels! At one point I tried to thank Senor Contreras. "Gracias, gracias," was about all that I could manage. He wouldn't let me thank him. Loosely translated, this is what he said to me. "Do not thank me. Thank God. I did not do this for you. I did it for Him." Wow! What could I answer? I couldn't, so I just did as he told me: I thanked God for providing the Contrerases for us.

Before we left C.A., we attended a memorial service. Afterward the principal told us that three little boys (two American and one Venezuelan) had come to know Jesus as Savior as a result of Mark's death. When he told me, I replied: "That is wonderful. I am so glad that some good has come out of Mark's death. Knowing that will make it easier for us." Outwardly, I said all the right things. Inside, I was screaming at God. Someone had to accept responsibility for Mark's death, and at the end of every avenue that my mind explored, I kept coming back to the fact that God had allowed Mark to die. Why hadn't He changed any one of the many circumstances and prevented Mark's death? I was so angry.

"God!" I cried. "You didn't need Mark to bring those boys to salvation. You are a great and a mighty God. You could have found another way. You didn't need my son!"

In the midst of my anger, I clearly heard the Lord reply, with disappointment in His voice, "But I sent My Son to die for you!" I was so ashamed. I had never realized the true significance of Jesus' death and resurrection. Because His Son died, I now had the promise of eternal life for my son. I didn't have to fear the grave. I could be sure that Mark was, at this very moment, alive and well with Jesus, and not alone, lying in the morgue. Later I also came to realize something else—there is a tremendous difference between God and myself. God gave His Son for me. I wouldn't have given my son for anyone.

We brought the body back to Louisville, Kentucky, where we had grown up and where our families still lived. They were all there to meet our plane and to share that moment. I never appreciated them any more than I did during the following days.

Every night we would lie awake, and every day we would say to ourselves: "I can't get through this day. I can't do the things that need to be done." And every day, the Lord would pick us up. He walked us through, putting people there to help whenever we needed them. Whenever a person would say, "I am praying for you," I knew that their prayers were the greatest gift that they could give to us. I truly was thankful because I knew that we would never get through this without God's help.

My anger began to subside, but a new emotion came to take its place. I felt guilty. I knew that Russ, Rusty, and I were suffering, but it was obvious that our family and friends were suffering also. By failing Mark, I had failed them. I was the mother. It was my responsibility to love and care for him and, of course, to protect him. Where did I fail? What if . . . ? Only questions, never answers, no chance to go back and change anything.

Later, Russ shared with me the guilt that he had felt. He had been serving in Viet Nam when Mark was born. He wasn't there for Mark's birth, and he wasn't there when Mark died. I'm sure that Rusty felt guilty because Mark was riding Rusty's skateboard at the time of the accident. What if . . . ? Was our guilt justified? Did it help in any way? No, it was only destructive.

God's Word was our greatest source of comfort. Right from the first, Russ and I had claimed Psalm 139 for ourselves. At first, we just claimed verses 1-5, particularly verses 3,5: "You chart the path ahead of me, and tell me where to stop and rest. . . . You both precede and follow me, and place your hand of blessing on my head." Later we claimed the entire chapter. I was especially blessed with verses 13-16. "You made all the delicate, inner parts of [Mark's] body, and knit them together in [his] mother's womb. . . . Your workmanship is marvelous—and how well I know it. . . . You saw [him] before [he] was born and scheduled each day of [his] life before [he] began to breathe. Every day was recorded in your Book" (TLB).

The Lord never failed. We made a lot of choices those days. We made them quickly. We made them decisively. Later I looked back and wondered at the wisdom shown in those decisions. Certainly, it was a wisdom greater than ours.

On the day of the funeral, it was as though I stood apart and had a private view. I could see the Lord at work and I knew that we were in His will. I felt severe pain, as well as a love greater than I could ever imagine. It was such a contradiction. "God, if You love us this much, why didn't You just let Mark live?" I still don't understand. Someday I will ask Him face to face, but for now, I have no choice but to accept it as God's will.

After the funeral, our return to Venezuela was delayed when Mr. Mabrey, Russ's seventy-year-old father, became ill and had to be hospitalized for the first time in his life. Death was a reality to us, and we feared for his life. Again, we turned to the Lord. "Please God, after all this family has just been through, we are too weak to take another tragedy." Mr. Mabrey returned home, and we were returned to Venezuela. But three months later, when we were all stronger, Mr. Mabrey joined Mark to live in heaven and to await the rest of the family.

The funeral was not the end. It was only the beginning. We had to go home and live normally, when nothing would ever be normal again. There was so much to be done and so many people to see. The people were the hardest. Although many people had come the night we received the news of Mark's death, many more had not. I knew that it was up to me to go to them. I tried to see them in a normal setting—a ladies' coffee or luncheon, language class, Bible study, church—even though I no longer had any real interest in being there. Everywhere I went, I could see the frozen smiles, or worse still, the downcast eyes, as I would enter the room. I was a freak! The unthinkable had happened to me—I had lost a child. I knew what they were thinking: "What if it had been my child?" They felt guilty. They were relieved that it was my loss and not their own. I knew how they felt because I, too, had felt that way when it had been someone else's child.

The hardest thing we did was to return to church. It was a very small congregation, about twenty people, so our arrival was noticed even though the service had already begun. Russ and I sat down and a hymn began. Hymns have a way of tearing away the exterior and exposing the heart. I felt the tears run down my face. I looked at Russ and found that he, too, had tears. I was embarrassed, so I looked to see if anyone was watching. To my great surprise, every person in the congregation was crying, men and women! They had known and loved Mark too. I'll never forget the love I felt for those people as the Body of Christ shared in our grief and suffering.

I continued to cry. I'm sure that I cried every day for two years. I decided that it was a good release, and I didn't deny it to myself. I was careful not to inflict my tears on others. Russ and Rusty dealt with their grief in other ways, and my tears would only cause them greater pain. So I took my tears and my anger to the Lord, and when I was feeling the sorriest for myself, He would remind me: "My Son died also. I have felt all of your pain and suffering. He died for you."

The pain that I felt was very physical. My body needed care, good foods, and plenty of rest. It was almost as though a giant monster had inserted its claws into my body and torn away a large part of my flesh. I felt exposed and vulnerable—in body and in spirit. I was well aware that Satan could easily destroy me and my family.

The psychology books clearly stated what I could expect—a serious physical illness, a mental breakdown, suicide, and very possibly, divorce. I was afraid, so again I turned to God. I was careful to allow only Christian books, music, and friends into my life while I was so weak. Maybe I went to extremes, but this was a matter of survival. God had promised in Philippians 4:13 that "I can do all things in Him who strengthens me" (RSV), and I needed to be strengthened!

It must have worked because in the next fourteen months, we did all of the things that those psychology books told us not to do. We moved from Venezuela back to our home in Michigan. Again there were people whom we hadn't seen since Mark's death. They were "waiting for us" so they could complete their own grieving process. It was very painful, but we received a lot of love.

My husband quit his job and went with a new company which meant that we would move again, this time to Nashville, Tennessee. Rusty changed schools twice, each time having to readjust and make new friends. God was so good to us during this time. It was interesting to see how He used Christians to accomplish things in our lives. The hardest part of our move was to answer the inevitable question that comes with meeting new people: "And how many children do you have?"

Throughout all of our experiences, Rusty's wishes had been an important consideration, and we included his suggestions whenever it was feasible. So, of course, he went with us when it was time to choose the grave marker. We chose a small angel for one corner, a rose for the other, "Beloved Son" at the top—easy, yet significant choices. Then Rusty asked if John 11:25-26 could be inscribed on the stone. Could it? Of course, it could! We were so pleased, and just a little embarrassed, that we had not thought of it ourselves.

Later, when I was alone and read the verses from my Bible, I was startled. Jesus was talking to Martha after Lazarus's death. She was in deep sorrow and was mourning. She had faith that Jesus was the Messiah, the Son of God, but she was disappointed that He hadn't arrived in time to prevent her brother's death. I could relate to her feelings! Jesus had been near to me during my sorrow and suffering. I knew that He was the Christ, but I, too, was disappointed that He hadn't acted to prevent the death.

Then Jesus stated plainly: "I am the resurrection and the life; he who believes in me, though he die, yet shall he live, and whoever lives and believes in me shall never die" (RSV). And then He asked her a question: "Do you believe this?"

I realized for the first time since Mark's death that this was the question I had been asking myself. Did I really believe this? I had thought I did. But if I did, why was I still so angry at God? I had turned to God, but not in total faith. Instead, I had been testing Him to prove that He really did love me and that all of those promises in His Word were true.

Before Mark's death, my faith had never been seriously tested. I had never questioned Jesus' death and resurrection; I had simply accepted it on faith. Suddenly, because of Mark's death, Jesus' death and resurrection had become the most important question in my life. I had to be sure. What did I really believe? Could I accept the fact that I had to let go and trust Mark's eternal life to Jesus Christ? God had given me my son; could I entrust Mark to God and gain needed peace and assurance?

God had given me no choice in the death of Mark's body. Although I had guided and influenced, only Mark had made his eternal choice. He had wisely chosen Christ. Now I had a choice to make. Would I hold on to my anger and guilt, nursing them into bitterness and self-destruction? Or would I accept Mark's death and praise God that He had worked in his young life, bringing him to salvation?

The Christian books I read following Mark's death had, it seemed to me, glibly suggested that all I had to do was to praise God and all my problems would disappear. I had been so angry. How could I praise God that my son was dead, that his future had been denied? Yet I knew instinctively I would never heal properly if I couldn't praise God again. I began to look for ways that I could honestly praise Him. Once I looked, they came in a flood.

I could praise God that He had loved us enough to give His son to die for our sins. Now I had the promise of eternal life for Mark, my family, other Christians, and myself.

I could praise God that I had lost my fear of death. Now I could anticipate it with joy.

I could praise God for His grace and the love that He gave in such abundance during our time of greatest need.

I could praise God for Christian family, friends, and others, many foreigners or people whom we had never met, who ministered to our basic needs of food, clothing, and shelter; who guided us through the miles of red tape necessary to return Mark's body to the United States; and especially for the hundreds of Christians, on at least two continents, who literally held us up in prayer when our own strength failed.

I could praise God for the mountaintop experience of walking and talking intimately with my God when I needed Him most. He never failed us.

Yes, I could praise God now more than I had ever been able to praise Him before, because my need had been great and He had been faithful.

Do I believe that Jesus is the resurrection and the life, that whoever believes in Him, though he die, yet shall he live, and whoever lives and believes in Jesus shall never die? Yes. I do believe this, and my prayer for you is that in your time of crisis, when your faith is tested, you, too, will be able to say "I believe!"

Diane Mabrey and her husband, Russ, were both raised in Louisville, Kentucky. They attended Valley High School. Afterward Diane graduated from Western Kentucky University in 1963 with a B.S. Degree and a teacher's certificate. She taught kindergarten and sixth grade for several years while living in Kentucky. Diane's talent in teaching has stood her in good stead as she has ministered to international women through church work and as she and Russ taught a Sunday School class for young married adults.

Russ was working for Ford Motor Company when they lived in Venezuela. After working for the Nissan Motor Manufacturing Corporation just outside of Nashville for five years, he and Diane have moved to the Detroit, Michigan area where he is employed by Chrysler.

Rusty was only thirteen months older than Mark. He was not present at Mark's death only because of some overwhelming feeling that he should stay behind and read a Christian book. Today he attends Oglethorpe University in Atlanta, Georgia, and is doing well.

5
Handicapped?!

by VIRGINIA ROSE "GINGER" GREENE

Me, handicapped? No, not really. I just have brittle bones. As a child I wondered why people saw me as "crippled"—that word I hate. Sure, I knew I was small, my chest protruded, and my legs were bowed, but so what? I was no different from anyone else. The people in "my world" treated me no differently, except, of course, for the many precautions and adaptations that were necessary. My family taught me I was lucky to have a good mind, and though my bones were very fragile, that did not affect my ability to be happy or my worth.

Born July 15, 1956, I was the third child of Chevius and Tressa Greene. They were excited to have a dainty little "Virginia Rose," more appropriately nicknamed "Ginger," to go along with their two rambunctious young boys, Tommy and Dicky. Three days later, however, the joy turned into agony. A broken arm was discovered, and upon further examination doctors found numerous broken ribs as well as evidence of earlier fractures which were now healed. They informed my parents that I had Osteogenesis Imperfecta (O.I.), commonly known as Brittle Bones. Doctors could tell them little about what to expect, except for the fact that I would have numerous fractures. Though it looked like I had a relatively mild case, my doctor suggested I would probably need to be raised in a crippled children's hospital. However, never ones to give up easily, my parents recovered from the initial shock and brought me home, determined to make my life as normal as possible.

Probably because of this attitude, my childhood contains many pleasant memories. I remember the neighborhood crawling races where my "alligator" knees, toughened by years of crawling, could outlast any of the other children's knees. I remember arguing with my brothers over whose potato chip was made from the biggest potato, and bragging about the value of having a cast on my arm to "clobber" them—though I don't recall them ever standing still long enough for me to use it! I remember starting first grade in a regular school with a cast on my leg, broken when our beloved family dog stepped on it, and the principal, E. Cassidy Bailey, coming out to the car and carrying me in each morning. I remember playing ping-pong while sitting on the table. I also remember the neighborhood children adapting almost any game they played so that I could play. In whiffle ball, I pitched and batted sitting down while teammates ran for me. While playing kick-the-can, I was always "It's" helper who stayed at the base and screamed to "It" that someone was coming! Children had a lot to offer concerning flexibility.

I also remember loving God and knowing He loved me. Jesus came into my heart just before my eleventh birthday after Rev. J. Ralph McIntyre spoke to the Vacation Bible School children. I remember very little about what Dr. McIntyre said, but I recall the excitement when I finally understood what it meant to accept Jesus and the elation I felt after I told Jesus I wanted Him to be my Savior and knew He was. Simple childlike faith sustained me through these years. I knew that with O.I. fractures often diminish as one approached puberty, so I always felt that someday I would walk. I knew God had His hands on my life, and I was happy.

One day a well-meaning person approached and said that she prayed daily that I would be healed. She suggested that I do the same. This horrified me! It had never occurred to me to pray daily for healing. I knew that God was aware that I wanted to be well. I felt that if healing was what He felt was best, He would do it. It seemed that my praying daily for a change would have produced daily dissatisfaction. As a child, I could not handle that. I was too busy coping with life as it was to be constantly thinking of what might have been or might be. I appreciated others' prayers for me, but for my part, I just had to leave it in God's hands. I was ready for a miracle when He was; but in the meantime, I was going to make the best of life as it was.

"But my God shall supply all your need according to His riches in glory by Christ Jesus" (Phil. 4:19) meant much to me as an adolescent. I began to struggle with who I was. The assurance that God loved and accepted me no matter what I was feeling sustained me. Life would be very different today had it not been for God's reassurance during this time.

One major area He helped me in was fear. As a child I often became sick at my stomach in the mornings before school. I did not associate this with fear then because I loved school and wanted to go. However, when I was a junior high school student, the problem worsened or at least became more exaggerated in my mind. I became sick being in new places without my parents or before doing anything unusual.

I could not control the problem, but by early high school, I realized it had to stop. I was becoming more physically independent—active in a club and sitting with friends in church—yet unbeknown to most friends, even these activities made me sick. I would not eat the last hour or so before going anywhere just in case the nausea appeared. It was very frustrating; yet I could not stop. Finally one day I told God I just could not handle it; He was going to have to help me. I realized I had to trust Him to take care of me and to take care of the nausea problem. That began the gradual healing process. Step by step He reassured me, and confidence was built. By the end of high school, not only was I able to go anywhere around town with friends; I went on a week-long mission trip with no problem at all.

During this junior and senior high school period, something else exciting was happening. I was gradually relearning to walk! I walked as a toddler, but then began breaking my right leg and was forced to get a brace which extended from heel to thigh and did not bend at the knee. Due to weakness and the weight of the brace, I could only walk very short distances and required someone holding my hand for support and balance. Most of the time I either rode a tricycle, crawled, or was carried. Then, at the age of eleven, I fractured my left leg and we purchased a wheelchair. Again, the next year my "good" leg was broken, while I was standing still in the school rest room. Reality was apparent—I must get a brace on this leg too. The wheelchair was not just a temporary device. However, God continued to lead.

When I went to be fitted for the brace on my left leg, the designer, Carlton Fillauer, told us about a new brace designed to support the weight from the knee. He thought it might enable me to walk. The orthopedist, however, was afraid to allow it, fearing another fracture. But with Mr. Fillauer's encouragement, my parents decided to try. "After all, she's not walking now," he told them. "What have you got to lose?" Because the brace was lightweight and extended only to the knee, it allowed more freedom of movement, yet there were no fractures. Two years later, the long brace on my right leg was replaced with the new type of brace, and I began relearning to walk. It was a slow process, but it was exciting! During college I became strong enough to walk wherever I chose—alone. God had led us. He had turned what we thought was tragedy (a fracture of my "good" leg) into triumph!

Then came career preparation; what a confusing time! Upon entering college I said there were two things I would never major in: music and education. Yes, you guessed it! Five years later, I had a B.A. in Music and a B.S. in Elementary Education.

I loved piano; however, I hated recitals. The thought of being in front of people, let alone to play the piano, was terrifying! Having stated the interest in piano on my college application, I was promptly assigned an adviser in the music department. At orientation I told him, in no uncertain terms, I was not going to major in music. I just liked to play the piano, but I was not going to continue taking piano lessons because I refused to be in any more recitals. He agreed, said I would not have to major in music or be in any recitals, yet proceeded to register me for music theory, sight singing, and piano! He proved to be the one person who could "out-stubborn" me anytime he chose to do so!

Piano juries (where the student plays for all the piano professors at the end of each semester) and the recitals provided a wonderful time for me to see the sufficiency of the Lord. (I was not "forced" to be in recitals, but between the encouragement of a professor and the urging of God to use what He had given me, it was difficult to refuse!) I had to come to the point of saying "This is for Your glory, Lord, not mine; if I mess up it's Yours; if I do well it's Yours." I still do not like recitals, but God proved that even there He is sufficient.

Still, I did not know what career to pursue. Though I loved music and saw its value as an emotional outlet, a good discipline, and a confidence builder, a career in it was not appealing to me. So, during those early years of college, in addition to music courses, I took a little of this and a little of that trying to determine a direction. One such course was orientation to teaching, which required aide work in a local elementary school. I liked it. Also, during each summer, I went on a mission trip with youth from my church and taught Vacation Bible School. No matter how hard I had fought it, I knew by the end of my junior year that I wanted to teach. Having finished the most difficult requirements of the music degree, I decided to complete it and stay the extra year required to obtain both the B.A. in Music and the B.S. in Elementary Education. Having fun in college another year sounded favorable, but where teaching was concerned there were doubts—How would I know what to teach? Could I control a classroom? Would the children be able to adapt? Yet I felt God was leading in that direction.

With preparations almost complete, the job search was ready to begin. I asked a professor whose opinion I valued if he thought I would have difficulty getting a job. "Yes," he bluntly replied. "But the schools that don't want you, you wouldn't want to teach in anyway." After teaching a few years I understood the wisdom of that statement. However, since I knew God wanted me to teach, I assumed He would simply "let a job fall in my lap." After a few interviews I discovered it was not going to be that easy! Preparing to teach and getting a job were two different things.

Many principals felt that my size (four feet tall and sixty pounds) would prohibit me from controlling a classroom, and I lacked the confidence, in spite of a good student teaching experience, to sell myself assertively. I thought I could do it, yet I had doubts. The more negative reactions I got, the more I doubted. At last, in midsummer, I walked into a positive interview. The principal, Patrick J. McMillen of Battlefield Elementary School, asked pertinent questions. "What is your philosophy of teaching? What problems brought on by your size did you encounter in student teaching, and how did you solve them? How do you deal with the children's curiosity about your condition?" Though he had no job openings, at the end of the interview he told me, "You are going to make someone a very good teacher." Those ten words provided an ocean of excitement and reassurance. Somebody believed in me. I was going to make it!

The weeks wore on; my doubts returned. The job I was *sure* would fall in my lap was not falling. I had felt, after the interview with Mr. McMillen, that I would be teaching at Battlefield Elementary in the fall. However, school started and I still had no job. This was a discouraging time. There were other interviews, but still no job. A friend pointed out Numbers 13—14, where Moses sent the spies into the Land of Canaan. Though the odds looked overwhelming, Joshua said in 14:8, "If the Lord delight in us, then He will bring us into this land." I could trust the fact that if God wanted me to teach, He would help me get a job. At last, in early October, Mr. McMillen called. One of his second grade teachers had had emergency surgery, and he needed a substitute for a month. I felt like shouting! At last I had an opportunity to prove myself. I was terrified on the first day, however, knowing that this was where I would sink or swim. But soon I loved it. After a few weeks I could not imagine myself doing anything but teaching.

The rest of the year I substituted there, filling in for two pregnancy leaves as well as many other sick days. The experience and confidence I gained were invaluable. In fact, I substituted in all the grades one through six and for every teacher except two. Soon after Christmas, Mr. McMillen told me the next job opening was mine. Sure enough, the next year a second grade opened up, and I began teaching full-time. The timing was not what I had planned, but the Lord was working. Once again, He had turned what I saw as a negative circumstance into one with positive results.

I do not think of myself as handicapped. Every person has areas in his life that he considers weaknesses. I realized as an adolescent, after fighting with my situation for a few years, that God loves me and accepts me as I am, and that is the least *I* can do, too. If I expect other people to accept me, I have to accept myself. Things come into each of our lives that we would not choose, but these "obstacles" are really opportunities. God said, "My strength is made perfect in weakness" (2 Cor. 12:9.). When we turn these obstacles over to Him, He is able to use them for His glory and to make our lives more fulfilling than we ever dreamed possible.

Virginia Rose "Ginger" Greene is a third-grade teacher at the Battlefield Elementary School in Ft. Oglethorpe, Georgia. She graduated magna cum laude from the University of Tennessee at Chattanooga in 1979 with a B.A. in Music and a B.S. in Elementary Education. She completed her M. Ed. in 1985. Ginger was named the 1981 Professional Handicapped Woman of the Year for the Tennessee District and an Outstanding Young Woman of America in 1984. She is an active member of Brainerd Baptist Church of Chattanooga, and the daughter of Chevius and Tressa Greene.

6
The Other Woman
by JENNY ABRAMS

The clock at my bedside read 3 AM. I knew by the way our car dug the gravel driveway that my husband had been drinking again. I had spent another sleepless night, and I was relieved to know he was finally home. The late hours, coupled with his drinking, had become a common thing in the last few months. I heard him fumble with the lock on the patio door and make his way toward our bedroom.

"Are you awake?" his voice was slurred. I pretended to be asleep and didn't answer. "Are you awake?" He persisted as he climbed into bed.

"Yes," I answered with faked sleepiness. I hoped he wouldn't be in one of his talkative moods. Experience had taught me it was better if he went to sleep as quickly as possible so he could sleep off the effects of the alcohol before time for work. This time he was too keyed up to go to sleep immediately.

"Don't you want to know where I've been?" he mumbled. He ignored my silence and spilled out the news I had tried to shield from my mind. John, in his liquor-induced condition, informed me he was seeing another woman. He had met Terri, who was also married, at his business. Soon their friendly relationship had turned into an affair.

I lay at his side long after he was fast asleep. Tears, which had been so near the surface all evening, coursed down my cheeks in the darkness. The ache of my heart encompassed my whole body.

My mind reflected on the past months. John had become increasingly critical of me, and it seemed nothing I did pleased him anymore. Now I wondered if his displeasure with me had been a cover-up for his own guilt.

I could understand another woman being attracted to my husband. It had been John's good looks which first attracted me to him ten years earlier.

I loved him almost immediately, and my love for him increased during the year we dated. He was a few years older than I, and I had deep respect for him. After we married, I became even more aware of his admirable traits. I admired his business ability. He was successful in his business, and everything he did seemed to prosper.

I admired John's appearance, his well-developed body, and his meticulous grooming. I was proud to be his wife. I knew other women were impressed, but I didn't mind. After all, he had chosen me as his wife.

When John and I married, neither of us were Christians. I accepted Christ as my Savior soon after Jimmy, our second son, was born. John ignored my new faith at first; then it became a source of irritation to him. I was becoming a better person as I grew in my faith, but he resented my "religion."

John gradually began to spend more and more evenings away from home. He said he was having dinner with his clients, and at first I believed him. Later these meetings began to spill over into the early morning hours. When I questioned him, he was evasive as to where he had been.

I discovered other things which added to my growing doubt about his nighttime activities: the smell of perfume in the car, a woman's cosmetic case under the seat of the car. When I confronted him, he tried to explain them away.

At first, I didn't want to face the truth of my suspicions. Now John had told me about the affair himself. I knew that when the effect of the alcohol wore off, he would be sorry he had told me.

I thought of Terri. Was she beautiful? Was she younger than

me? What had attracted John to her? Did she visit my husband's business often during the day?

Suddenly I felt unattractive. I was conscious of the extra pounds that had remained after the birth of my last baby. My hair needed a new perm. I thought of the clothes I wore long after they were no longer attractive. My whole attention had been directed toward being a wife and mother, and I had neglected my appearance.

Terri had hurt me deeply, so I wanted to hurt her in return. In my anger, I visualized what I would do to her if I met her. At that moment, I could have pulled her hair out by the roots.

A wave of anger welled up inside me against John. How could he spend our money on liquor and another woman when I denied myself things I needed? *As soon as he wakes up,* I decided, *I'll insist on money to go shopping for new clothes. I might even buy a new kitchen range.*

Then I reasoned, *What good are new clothes if the one you love doesn't love you? What joy can a new kitchen range bring, if the one you are cooking for loves somebody else? To get money from John because of his guilt wouldn't be right.*

John turned in his sleep and put his arm around me. For a moment I drew myself close to him. *Maybe I'll wake up and find I'm having a bad dream,* I thought. *John will take me in his arms and tell me he loves me, as he has done so many times before.* But my mind forced me back to reality. This time I wouldn't wake up. This nightmare was real.

A struggle raged inside me. I was drawn to John, and repulsed at the same time. A part of me wanted to snuggle up to him and let him love me and make everything all right. Another part of me wanted to recoil from his touch. Suddenly his embrace felt dirty. The love I had shared with him was now defiled.

My mind traveled like a car out of control. Did he think it was Terri in the bed with him? How many times in the last year had he imagined he was with Terri instead of me? Did he compare our lovemaking? Suddenly I felt self-conscious. How did I compare to her?

When John awoke, he seemed to be truly sorry for the pain he had brought on me. He took me in his arms and asked me to forgive him. I cried. I don't know if it was my tears or his guilty conscience, but he tried to reassure me that he loved me and that Terri didn't mean anything to him. I believed him because it was what I wanted to hear.

But John didn't stop seeing Terri. Neither did he deny it anymore. Now he no longer tried to keep his visits with Terri secret. It became a regular occurrence for him to come home from work, take a bath, and go out for the evening with Terri.

"Mama, why doesn't Daddy stay and play with me?" My young son watched his daddy leave for his regular date with Terri. David's tearful eyes searched my face for an answer. My heart ached for him. I couldn't explain to my five-year-old that his daddy was seeing another woman.

"Daddy had to go somewhere," I replied as I pulled David close to me. I felt comfort from his small body as I fought to choke back the tears which rimmed my eyes. In a few minutes he wriggled free from my embrace and ran out to play with his new puppy.

Jimmy, almost three, climbed up into my lap. He looked into my face, unable to understand the tears he saw in his mommy's eyes. I drew him close, thankful for his cuddly body next to mine. The torrent of tears, which I couldn't hold back any longer, spilled over into his hair beneath my chin. It would be another long night alone.

I don't know why I didn't leave John, except that when I married him, I took him for better or worse. I believe that marriage is forever, or until one marriage partner dies. I loved him very much, and I hoped that John would someday love me again.

Even if I left John, where would I go? I had no close family. I couldn't leave without my children, and I didn't want to take them away from their father. John loved his sons, and he was good to them. In his weak way, he loved me, too. For the sake of our children, I decided to stay and make our home as happy as possible.

In the days that followed, there was a deep hurt inside me constantly. It was like someone thrusting a knife into the innermost part of my heart and twisting it. In my emotions, there was a grief I couldn't overcome. Tears, which were always near the surface, spilled over many times, especially as I poured out my feelings in prayer to my new friend, Jesus Christ.

Jesus said, "Come to me, all you who are weary and burdened, and I will give you rest" (Matt. 11:28, NIV). I found His rest. In my pain, God gave me peace that was past understanding. He gave me joy in the midst of my sorrow. This enabled me to cope with the pressures I faced each day.

Nagging John about his love affair got me nowhere. He only found more fault with me. I soon learned it was more peaceful not to mention Terri to him. When I was able to commit everything to God, the load was easier. If I let my mind dwell on how bad things were, soon I was in the pit of despair.

When John left in the evenings to see Terri, I would usually put the kids to bed and then spend the time praying and reading my Bible. My weak faith began to grow as I received God's comfort and strength.

God was turning my difficult circumstances into training sessions in biblical truths. He said to me from his Word, "It is mine to avenge; I will repay" (Rom. 12:19, NIV). It wasn't easy for me to learn the lessons of faith in God, but ever so slowly God enabled me to turn my desire for vengeance over to Him.

There was another inner problem I hadn't faced yet. One day, as I was going about my housework, God spoke to my heart. *You haven't forgiven Terri.*

But, Lord, I replied, *look what she has done to me.*

She has wronged you, but your unforgiveness is also sin. I wrestled with God's Word, trying to rationalize my situation. *I have the right to hold her guilt against her,* I reasoned. *She's guilty of adultery, and God's Word condemns it.*

God reminded me that the same Word that condemns adultery also instructs us to love our enemies and to do good to those who do us evil. I began to see things from God's perspective. Adultery is a sin in God's sight, but so is unforgiveness. From God's perspective, I, too, was guilty. He didn't condone her sin; neither did he excuse mine. If I wanted to please God, I must forgive. I knew I should forgive, but I couldn't. I prayed for God's power in my life, and God enabled me to forgive Terri.

My life continued to be a struggle between the truth of God's Word and my own human emotions. I wanted to call Terri's husband. *Surely,* I reasoned, *I should tell him his wife is having an affair with my husband. But what if he became violent and killed my husband and his wife? My children could be deprived of their father, and it would be my fault.* I decided against it.

I read in my Bible about David and King Saul. Saul was trying to kill David, but David didn't kill Saul even though he had a good chance to do so. Instead, he left the whole matter in God's hands (1 Sam. 24). If it worked for David, surely it would work for me. God gave me the strength to wait for God's deliverance.

Meanwhile, the affair went on and the hurt continued. As I read my Bible daily, its words became precious to me. Many times when the future looked dark and I felt I could go no further, God's words revived me. I prayed often for God's strength.

I also prayed for the salvation of my husband. God made me aware that my husband was living in the power given him by his master, Satan. I couldn't expect him to live the Christian life without accepting Jesus Christ, who is the power of that life. God assured me in my heart that he would someday become a Christian.

I wish I could say that God immediately answered my prayer to restore my home and that we all lived happily ever after. But it didn't end that way. God did give me joy in the midst of my problem and grace to endure the hardships. He gave me a special love for my unfaithful husband and an understanding of God I would never have had except for my trial.

John divorced me and married his lover. Just as the ancient prophet Job, I came out better than before. Those hard times I experienced have worked in my life to make me a happy and fulfilled woman. The happiness I have now is built on the foundation of faith in God that I learned in those hard days. I can say with Joseph in the Old Testament that, in my trying times, "God intended it for good" (Gen. 50:19).

Jenny Abrams is involved in her local church as a Sunday School teacher, where she has taught for thirty-five years. She is a free-lance writer and has contributed to many national magazines. She is the mother of two sons.

7
Understanding My Aging Mother

by JUNE HOLLAND McEWEN

She looked at me from beneath heavy brows out of glittering brown eyes. "No, I'll not do it," she said firmly and loudly. Her mouth set in a straight stubborn line as she bit off the end of each word as though tearing off a strand of sewing thread. Breathing deeply and deliberately, I counted to three and tried once more to persuade her to do a simple action that would make life easier for her and for me. But to no avail.

Does this kind of exchange remind you of trying to persuade a stubborn and willful child? Of trying to contain anger and to keep self-control? Well, the situation could easily be a mother dealing with a strong-willed child, but the fact is that the scene took place between me and my aging mother.

At what point do roles reverse and grown children suddenly find themselves being parent to their mother or father? How do both parties deal with such role reversals? How can care and protection be provided, and at the same time allow the aged parent to maintain self-respect and self-control?

How does the mature child do what the Bible commands and still have time for her own life, her own family, and also keep her emotions under control? "Honor thy father and thy mother that their days may be long upon the earth" sounds easy. It sounds like something all human beings can and will do as a natural response to the parent who gave them life, who nurtured them when they were young and helpless.

But, like so much in life, what seems easy, natural, and obvious is sometimes difficult, demanding, and trying. For some children, caring for parents is almost altogether a duty.

For me several factors made caring for my mother extremely difficult. First, she was a semi-invalid who absolutely refused to consider any situation other than living alone. It fell my lot in my family to be primary caregiver at this particular time. The others took turns either at earlier or later times. We are a large family, and all were willing to share responsibilities. This is a blessing for which I continually give thanks.

My mother seemed especially to resent me and my having any say about her affairs—a delicate situation which was a trial to both her and me. Added to this was the fact that I had moved about three hundred miles away and thus had to do a great deal for her by telephone or automobile or bus trips. Somehow we managed to get everything done: visits to the dentist and doctor, paying the bills, and doing the shopping. Too often the most simple actions became occasions for struggle between us. I was determined that she would do things a certain way, and she was just as determined she would do them another way.

One day our mutual stubbornness reached a stalemate. I stormed angrily from her tiny apartment after her tight-lipped refusal and adamant assertion, "I will not do it." I drove away in a state of deep despair and hopelessness.

Suddenly I realized the nature of our situation. She needed desperately to hang on to the last thing that was left to her as a sick, nearly helpless, aging woman. Her self-determination, her independence, her control of her life—these were all she had left.

My mother had not only refused to order her activities the way I wanted; she had said to me, "If only I had a car, then I'd do as I please." The vision of her driving a car was ludicrous. How could she even get herself in and out of the driver's seat? How could her limited budget stand the added expense that car ownership and maintenance require? These practical matters crowded my mind. Then too, she would be a danger on the road—to herself and to others. Even worse, I would have no idea where she was or what she was doing.

At the last thought a light burst in my understanding! It was this that I feared. I would not know where she was or what she was doing. She would be out of my range. It is an unpleasant thing to see yourself in such a bad light. To admit to being selfish is not easy, but driving along in the coolness and quiet of that autumn day, I was confronted with a view of myself that was hard to accept.

With the truth before me, I knew I would have to face changes in both what I did and how I went about doing it. This was an occasion to call on the Father for help. Strength, resourcefulness, forgiveness, and encouragement are readily available once a Christian stops still and allows God and the truths of His Word to permeate mind and spirit.

Thus, a new vision for what I must do and what I wanted to do began to take shape. Returning to the apartment, I started afresh to do the myriad daily routine deeds that helping a shut-in involves.

All the while I was demanding that she be docile and obedient and make things easy and smooth for me so that I might discharge my responsibilities as quickly and as efficiently as I could. I wanted to do what I needed to for her and then to get on with my own life, my own affairs. Her need for self-esteem interfered with my plans.

The awful thought flashed through my head as I drove along, *I want to control my mother. I want to tend to her needs quickly and mark that off my list of things to get done.* Suddenly I saw not just her willfulness, her stubbornness, not just her being a duty in my day, but as a person, an individual—more than just my mother.

True, she was my responsibility, my duty. But she was also a precious individual, a personality, a person of worth regardless of age or health. I saw her in my imagination as the young, black-haired girl who loved the Charleston, flapper styles, laughter, and good times. She was the young mother who dressed my brother and me in matching sailor suits and proudly showed us off. Her tiny frame, now restrained to endless hours in the confinement of the shiny, stainless steel wheelchair, once bustled about the kitchen, peeling and preserving peaches and beans, and making constant meals for six small children. Her strength had been pitched against the demands of cleaning, cooking, and caring for us for year after year. Now her area of activity was so constrained, so limited.

To look at the white hair, the olive skin now lightly etched with the lines of the years, the frail body, the nearly useless legs, one had to use the eyesight of love and imagination to see what it really means to become old and to be helpless and dependent on others. Thus the right to decide and to choose becomes infinitely precious. This is the last power we relinquish to the relentless on-rush of age. No wonder my mother set her jaw and spat out her defiant words, "No, I'll not do it."

The fact was that I had wanted her at one stage to agree to a walker in place of a crutch that no longer was steady and safe. Later I insisted that the wheelchair would be better for safety and for mobility. All this was so sensible and obvious to me. But what seemed obvious to me represented something entirely different to her. With each accommodation she was letting go of another significant amount of her independence. For each stage of what was security and common sense to me, she was less and less a free person in charge of herself.

Driving along, the realization of what was happening to both of us settled clearly in my mind. Slowly, an entirely different approach for dealing with her began to form.

I would suggest possibilities and options, and then allow time for her to choose and to make her own decisions in her own way.

I would be more patient while she took the time to think over these matters which were of central concern to her.

I would work with situations that suited her even though this would often add to my inconvenience and use more of my time.

I would agree to more of her ideas, ways, and opinions even though they seemed wasteful or wrong-headed to me.

In sum, I would see this little woman as a human being who had hopes and dreams, who was a person quite distinct and apart from being my mother. I would treat her with consideration and courtesy and listen to what *she* wanted rather than do what was easiest or most convenient for me.

A great help in my new resolve was found in a book by M. Scott Peck, *The Road Less Traveled*. Dr. Peck defines love as an act of the will, a way of self-discipline. It is his view that we must have the courage to do the right thing. He asserts that we love when we attend to the spiritual nurture of another person. This course of action was the course I set for myself. I would have the courage and the will to love and to honor my mother by seeking her spiritual nurture before my own ease and convenience.

This kind of resolve is aided immeasurably by maintaining a sense of proportion and an awareness of the limits of time. I began to make the most of opportunities to laugh with my mother. She would often joke about her slowness of movement. I joined her in her wry sense of fun. We began to remind each other that her plight was not as bad as it could have been. We both knew without framing the words that the work we were doing together was of a limited duration under the best of circumstances. Time would run out. It became easier to concentrate on the here and the now. The words of an old Vacation Bible School motto became my watchword: "I will do the best I can with what I have where I am for Jesus' sake today."

To have the will, the discipline, and the courage to act in a loving manner to one's parent is a gift to be earnestly sought. The eased relationship and joy in being together is increased and the discharging of duties is made more pleasant for both.

For a Christian it is essential that we love, honor, and respect one another as Christ taught and as He demonstrated. What better time, person, and place for such love and honor than in the relationship to an aging parent?

These attitudes and actions can and must be lived and practiced regardless of the past relationships between parent and child. Those admonitions can be met regardless of circumstances, of judging how good a job one's parent may have done, of how deeply affectionate one feels or does not feel. A Christian can have the will and the discipline to be obedient to God's command, "Honor thy father and thy mother."

This kind of honor requires the courage and the will to nurture one's own soul as well as caring for the physical, emotional, and spiritual needs of aging parents.

June Holland McEwen, a native of Kingston, Tennessee, is an honor graduate of the University of Chattanooga and holds the Master of Education degree from the University of Tennessee at Chattanooga. She has taught English at both the high school and college levels, served as executive director of the Chattanooga YWCA, and held administrative positions in both private and public educational institutions.

A free-lance writer, she has written articles for a variety of educational and religious publications. An editor of and contributor to the book, *Women on Pilgrimage*, she has also written a book on her own, *The Gift of Simplicity*, both Broadman releases.

Currently Mrs. McEwen is assistant to the director of the Brock Scholars/Honors Program at the University of Tennessee at Chattanooga. Her work is in the area of student recruitment, advising, planning, and coordinating in the honors program.

8
Moving Into Faith
by AVERIL PETERS

We made the move to our West Tennessee home on a terrifically hot day. As we left our beloved ranch-style home near Bristol in Eastern Tennessee on that August day, the weather was not a matter of concern. We gloried in the sweetness of the clear, early morning air as our two-vehicle caravan left the high altitude plateau in the South Holston Mountain area. The heat came as a pressing blanket later in the day in the low altitude western land to which we were headed.

We were aiming toward adventure! My husband, Pete, led the way in the large old black paneled truck which we had packed to the "gills" with as many of our household furnishings as we could press into it. I drove behind him in the little tan stationwagon, "Hilda," that had served us so well in other adventures. Dear little Hilda nestled close to the pavement under her load of houseplants, bedding, dishes, our teenage children, Brian and Jennifer, three dogs, and a five-week-old pig.

The other members of the small pig herd that we owned would have to come later. It would take nine more trips before the move would be completed. Little "Miss Kitty" had become a lovable part of our menagerie, so it was unthinkable that she should be left behind. You see, Miss Kitty was a little orphan Duroc pig who had never known her mother. It was to humans that she went for her food, comfort, and loving.

Riding in a car was new to Miss Kitty and was not a common practice for the three dogs, so frequent rest stops were necessary.

We derived great amusement from viewing the startled expressions on the faces of other resting travelers as we paraded past them to the water faucets with a large Weimaranar dog, two small hairy-faced dogs, and a little red pig—all on leashes and behaving themselves admirably.

Nearly 480 miles and many hours later, we arrived just at dusk at what we were now considering our pioneer home. A hurried unpacking of mattresses and bedding was accomplished in the gathering dark. The dogs and Miss Kitty were comforted and reassured that their placement in an old dilapidated chicken house was only temporary until we could furnish them with more luxurious quarters.

That hot August day was the beginning of a new life that we were planning to carve out for ourselves. Pete had taught as a professor of the sciences at Sullins College on the Virginia side of the twin city of Bristol, Virginia-Tennessee. For eleven years, life seemed idyllic as our association with the small two-year girls' college allowed Pete to expand his teaching talents. He had previously taught for eight years on the high school level and then he was challenged and rewarded with the cleverness of girls in this higher learning situation.

Our children barely had known any other life than that their Daddy taught at a college. They were allowed all of the privileges of extracurricular activities that the college girls enjoyed: horseback riding, ballet lessons, music lessons, theater work, musical and theatrical performances, and hearing visiting lecturers.

Then the college closed. Its many years of operating as a finishing school for young ladies had expanded to include a very fine curriculum for serious-minded girls. However, the gentle Southern style of gracious living that was the background atmosphere for the college didn't prepare the college officials for the aggressive push of the community colleges. Sullins College gave a gentle sigh of defeat and closed its doors in 1976.

Pete and I had a farm life upbringing, and farming has always been in our blood. So far, however, it had been expressed only through gardening and a few years that Pete spent in swine production on a small scale, plus the effort of raising a few crops on rented land. The front half of our small plot of 3 1/2 acres was tended to its limits with a section for garden, a section planted in fruit and nut trees, a fairly large hip-roofed barn of Pete's design and construction, and a spreading lawn surrounding our brick ranch-style home. The back half of this tiny acreage was given to the lots and buildings necessary for our small swine herd.

With the experience in farming that we had, it seemed only natural that our thoughts for another way of life should turn to farming. We knew that our monetary resources would not allow for outlay on a ready-made farm, so we looked for a neglected one that we could build up ourselves with God's help in providing the wisdom, strength, and perseverance that would be needed to see us through.

We had begun this plunge into adventure with prayer and the desire that this was God's will for us. With the belief that this was, indeed, God's will, we began the restructuring of an old, run-down, and neglected farm in the outlying 'boonies' of Henry County, near the friendly little village of Cottage Grove, Tennessee.

Sounds simple, doesn't it? That is why I couldn't forgive myself for my ambivalent feelings. I knew in my head and heart that this was God's will for us, and yet I found myself in unhappiness so many times. I knew that we had planned excitedly to begin a life of what we referred to as "pioneering" and that it would not be an easy life; yet I found myself yearning for the old life. I knew that we had talked the decision over with the children and that they were enthused, too. Yet I felt guilty about uprooting them from the only friends and way of life that they had known.

Jennifer's enthusiasm was barely existent; however, we tried to bolster it a bit with the promise that at her new home she would have the much desired horse of her very own. It seemed logical that we would have plenty of space on a farm of over one hundred acres. Space was available; however, we soon found that money resources and time were not. All of our efforts had to be centered around providing for the hogs, which were supposed to make our living for us. The purchase of the horse and the time for constructing a fence for it would have to wait.

The hogs were brought with the very next load of belongings to be transferred those many miles from East to West Tennessee. Swine are easily overheated, so they were brought at night. There were some thirty-odd creatures that landed on this heat-satiated soil. We made every effort that we could think of to make them comfortable. To our dismay, our prize boar died of heat stroke on the first day. My feeling of guilt took over again. A beautiful animal had been stricken in a horrible way because he couldn't readily adjust to the change in climate.

The children fitted into their new school system easily in the academic category. They each had made fine grades and were ideal students with their innate desire to learn. Discipline had never been a problem. This part of the transition was pleasantly satisfactory.

However, my guilt bugaboo rose again to gigantic proportions when Jennifer's sixteenth birthday arrived in January. If we had remained in our Bristol home, there would have been quite an exciting party planned for her. In fact, Jennifer and I had talked about what wonderful things would be done on this special birthday anniversary. The party would include any and all of her several girl friends. Since she was naturally a gregarious youngster with a sweet, friendly disposition, I was agreeably resigned to the fact that there would be more young voices chattering and squealing their excitement at the party than the sturdy roof of our home could contain.

The stark fact, as her birthday approached, was that this delightful child had formed no serious friendships that would entice her to plan eagerly again for this very important occasion. One or two girls who worshiped at the same church we did were fun for her to be with and had been visitors in our home; but there were none of those lifelong friends with whom Jennifer had shared so many secrets and pleasures of growing up. Although I encouraged Jennifer to make some alternate and, hopefully, exciting plans, she insisted that she would just as soon not try to plan a large party. The oh-so-special sixteenth birthday was spent quietly as an evening out with her family.

Apparently, most boys are fairly self-contained in nature. At least, Brian seemed to take the change in location and friends a little better in stride. Then, too, this senior year in high school brought its own excitement, with plans for college life in the near future. There were many decisions to make for the life that he wanted to lead after high school graduation. Would he be accepted into the Naval Academy? Would his ACT and SAT tests accurately reflect the degree of education that he had received? What college would he attend if he didn't attend the Naval Academy? These matters kept him always planning ahead, with ever-lessening thoughts spent on the used-to-be.

An event occurred that put a shine on the whole first year in the new home for him. It was Brian's opportunity to be a part of National 4-H Club Competition. The week that he spent in Chicago, Illinois as a delegate from Tennessee was culminated with the thrilling realization that he was a national winner in his Entomology project. Newspaper cover stories of this accomplishment and the resulting congratulations from people all about him made this a pretty exciting period of his life.

Slowly, progress was made on the farm. Buildings were constructed, new fencing was erected, and improvements were made on the old farmhouse that had become our home.

We still laughingly recall the event that became the impetus for remodeling the front room. Jennifer was deep in study of one of the subjects she was taking in high school. As she read American History and tried to absorb the material, she absentmindedly tapped the wall at the end of the couch with her finger. All of a sudden, her finger went through the wall! Of course, she was dumbfounded

Upon examination, we discovered that the wall consisted of plain cardboard tacked onto the upright studs. This, then, had been covered with wallpaper for what seemingly was a finished room. Obviously, the former owners had "made do" with whatever was at hand in the construction of this oddly built house. In view of the winter yet to be faced, it seemed like a good idea to set aside some time and money for refinishing the front room with the proper insulation and materials.

We are a family who naturally loves to laugh, so we can recall many laughter-provoking occasions during those early years. For instance, there was the time that Pete and I tried to usher a heavily pregnant sow into the new farrowing barn for the arrival of her baby pigs. We had driven her from her outside pen to the barn. There were several rushing side trips that the sow insisted upon taking in her confusion, so the move to the barn was not without struggle. However, we finally got close to the open door of the barn. Light emanated from the opening. The smell of feed wafted on the air to entice her. Warmth from within beckoned to her on that chilly winter day.

As she stuck her head through the door, we considered that the struggle was over. Not so. She whirled, quick as a wink, and raced back the way she had come. Pete was just behind her, but before he could realize that the stubborn sow had changed her mind, he found himself riding the sow backward! She rushed at him so hard that her head thrust between his legs, and off she went, with him astraddle of her leaping back. Pete rode that sow with all of the aplomb of a professional cowboy for several mighty leaps, landed on his feet, and whirled to block the sow's escape. I had to hide my chuckles behind a gloved hand. Pete was not exactly in a good humor at that time, even though he has given his crooked grin several times since, in response to our teasing remembrances of the episode.

Oh, yes, we had some light-hearted times working together at this pioneering adventure. We were not afraid of work, and it was exciting to plan for the next improvement to be made. Thank the

Lord's goodness, we were blessed with excellent health, a sense of family unity, and a precious love for one another.

As far as Pete was concerned, this was the land of "milk and honey." We had over one hundred acres of mostly wooded land on which he could indulge in his favorite hobby of hunting. Deer were plentiful. Squirrels were bouncing in the trees. Rabbits and quail scattered seemingly everywhere. Before long, several farm ponds were teeming with fish to satisfy another hobby of fishing. Pete worked very hard . . . and played hard.

Before the year was out, Jennifer formed some good friendships. Through the guidance of an able teacher, she discovered that she was very adept in various art forms. The praise and admiration that she received over her painting and pottery gave her a sense of personal satisfaction.

My family had made their adjustment to the new life. Basically, I had, too. It was my custom to seek reassurance from a favorite verse of the Psalms, "This is the day which the Lord has made;/Let us rejoice and be glad in it" (Ps. 118:24, NASB). I quoted this to myself often as I went about my daily routine to reassure myself that God was in control, even though the desired goal for the farm seemed far away.

I am not a person who is easily given to weeping; however, there were so many adjustments to be made in this new land in contrast to the former life that I found myself breaking into tears of sudden consternation over the drab conditions of our farm. It seemed to take forever to shape our house and land into a semblance of order and beauty. I missed our former church family, which constituted the bulk of the friendships we had made in East Tennessee. (The members of the new church family were so loving and supportive, though, that we had no trouble feeling a part of the community.) Whereas we had been accustomed to well-paved roads, we now had to become resigned to the fact that the dirt road connecting our land to civilization was going to be choking with dust in the summer and hardly passable with mud in the winter.

Our former home had been all that I wanted in design. The house that we now were trying to make into a home had much to be desired as far as space and design. I had been used to the sweep of a beautifully contrasting landscape of mountains on one side of our former home and spreading valley on the other side. The fields were lush with a vibrant green, summer and winter, in that high altitude land. In our new location, we were closed in with woods on each side of us. I enjoy trees, but their denseness made me feel claustrophobic. We had to adjust to land that grew stale and brittle in the excessive heat of summer and that became gray and drear in the starkness of winter.

Then came spring to renew our spirits. We discovered, constantly, in those awakening months, the beauty that delighted us on our Woodsgift Farm. Flowers of so many varieties sprang up from the warming soil that we obtained a field guidebook with which to identify them. Ferns grew lushly in many places throughout the woods. One spot that seemed carpeted with the graceful plants became known as "Fern Valley."

Individual trees in our densely populated woods were so majestic that they became a means of identifying that area. There was the King Oak, with his court of surrounding cedar trees. There was the Queen Oak, with her dogwood ladies-in-waiting. Then, there was Dogwood Valley with its snowy canopy of shining blossoms.

During the frequent walks that Pete and I took over our land, I was as enchanted at the realization that we owned this hilly, wooded land as he was. The exploring of each nook and cranny became a means of relaxing from the rigors of our work schedule.

Even though, in the next couple of years, our life sorted itself out to a more comfortable schedule, and even though I remained in the conviction that our move was in God's plan for us, I still had distressing moments of turmoil. As a result, I felt that I was letting God down in my strong desire to be faithful to Him and His plan for our lives. Why couldn't I be more patient and contented with the realization that progress was being made . . . and at a reasonable rate?

Finally, something that the minister said during a Sunday morning's sermon came to me as an understanding of the real reason for my spurts of unhappy longing. I was experiencing grief! I was simply grieving through a stressful change from one fulfilling way of life into one that had yet to prove itself. Since the Lord experienced grief in a very real way while He was on earth, I am comforted in the belief that God understands my very human emotions and will patiently uphold me. "Weeping may last for the night,/But a shout of joy comes in the morning" (Ps. 30:5*b*, NASB).

Averil Peters lives in Cottage Grove, Tennessee, with husband Pete on Woodsgift Farm. She has a weekly column, "Simply Sharing," in the *Paris Post-Intelligencer*, the local newspaper. Son Brian is a conscientious student at the University of Tennessee—Martin, and daughter Jennifer teaches high-school Spanish in Gate City, Virginia. Averil sees life as an exciting adventure and carries a spark of that excitement with her in every endeavor.

9
My Husband's Drug Problem

by FRAN JONES SNYDER

It was a cold, winter day in November 1961. Whipping around our little frame house, the wind challenged the tiny structure to yield to its mighty strength. The meager heat the old furnace was putting out was not enough to keep the house warm. Tonight, inside was almost as cold as outside.

My day at the office had been difficult, and I was weary. I had not regained my strength from a bout with pneumonia. But it was not the cold wind, the partially working furnace, or even the weariness that was nagging at my emotions as I prepared the evening meal. It was the scene of my husband sprawled across the bed. He had passed out hours before. I prayed that he would sleep until morning so the children would not be upset again tonight. My husband used drugs. What I dreaded most about his drug use and drug "binges" was what always happened after he awakened. There would be an outburst of foul language, abusive threats, and, lately, physical abuse. Thank God, he had never physically harmed the three boys during his rages. But it was bad enough for them to be exposed to his irascible moods. He had been diagnosed as schizophrenic, a mental disease that causes sudden and severe mood changes. His habitual use of drugs, coupled with the schizophrenic symptoms, created an environment in our home equal to a time bomb.

I had made my decision. Earlier that day, I had decided I could not put off any longer taking steps to get our precious children away from this environment. It would not be like the other times we left, and came back after he had promised there would be no more drugs. This time I would file for a divorce.

Divorce—The very word made me flinch. Could I go against my Christian beliefs and get a divorce? I hated the thought, but we had tried everything else. Nothing had worked. All those months he had spent in the state mental hospital and the year in the federal narcotics hospital had not made any difference in his habit. I felt there was no other way.

Later that evening I knew my decision was right. He awakened and went into the worst rage we had yet experienced. He locked all the doors, herded us into the bedroom, and made us sit on the bed. He was completely out of control. He picked up an empty soft-drink bottle, walked the few steps to the kitchen, and, holding it by its neck, struck the bottom against the edge of the cabinet. The bottle shattered, leaving an ugly, jagged edge. *Oh, dear God,* I thought as he walked back toward the bedroom. *He plans to use it as a weapon.* I was petrified! The children were screaming! (Our ten-year-old had gone to a Boy Scout meeting. I thanked God at least one of us would survive!) I frantically began to think of a way to get the other two children out of the house, but it was too late.

He picked up the alarm clock and declared that he was setting it for thirty minutes. When the alarm went off, he said, he would kill us—and then himself. He pulled up a chair and sat facing us with the jagged-edged bottle in his hand. I was so horror-stricken I could scarcely breathe. I pleaded with him—but to no avail. He kept lamenting his need to "end it all." He reminded us every few minutes how much time we had left. He was like a mad animal.

I held our precious little boys close to me, the two-year-old in my lap and the five-year-old beside me. Their sobs were tearing out my heart, but I could not calm their fears or their hysteria. The only thing I could do was hold them close—and pray.

By the grace of God, his threats were never carried out. When the alarm went off, he slammed the bottle to the floor with a force that shattered it into a thousand pieces, and stalked out of the room.

I have no memory of how I calmed the children that night and got them to sleep—only that I sat by their bed all night and prayed.

In the morning we slipped out of the house while he slept, and I made the necessary arrangements to have him hospitalized.

(Dear God, remind me to never give up hope in You—to know, when everything is falling apart around us and there seems to be no hope, that You are there. You are always there with love to surround us and comfort us and to give us new hope.)

I filed for the divorce. It was very painful, but it was the only thing left to do. I prayed it would bring an end to the hopeless trauma our lives had been for the past few years. It would give the children a chance at life. It would be a new beginning.

During the months of waiting for the final decree of the divorce, I had many reflections of what our marriage had been like. There had been many happy times, but they were so punctuated by episodes with drugs that it was hard to remember them. I thought back in time to the beginning of our marriage. Surely, there would be some happy memories there. I needed some of those to hold onto. The boys would need to remember the happy times, so I would store them up in my memory, and someday I would present these to them as a gift. This would be one of the gifts.

The monitor light came on in the radio station sound booth, indicating the one-minute countdown to end the program. I made the necessary adjustments to the stops on the organ and began playing the refrain of our theme song. My husband and I both loved doing the radio program; it was exciting and fulfilling, and music was a very important part of our lives. We each had made commitments to God long before we met and married. I listened as my husband sang the beautiful, inspirational words. He was in fine voice. He almost always was. He had that special quality to his voice that was magnetism. It matched his warm, tender, and compassionate personality of those early years. It was attested again that day by the radio listeners who called in to say, "Thank you for sharing your songs of faith that touched our lives today." We thanked them and God for allowing us this privilege.

The radio program was the reality of one of our dreams to fulfill our commitment to God. But after a few months, my husband decided to give up the program. There was no reasonable explanation. He simply folded up our music and walked out of the studio and away from our dream. His moods were becoming more and more irascible and it was apparent that a personality change was taking place. This was the first real indication he gave me that he had a problem with drugs.

Divorce! The day came when my final divorce decree was handed to me. I was shocked at the emotional impact I experienced. Convulsive, uncontrollable sobs, starting in the pit of my stomach, ripped through my chest and tore at my throat as I read the legal document labeled "Divorce." *My* divorce! From my husband of thirteen years. The agony of it was crushing the air from my lungs. I could not breathe. I was hurting, deeper than any hurt I could remember.

How could God let this happen to me? I asked. Why didn't He intervene? Why didn't He work a miracle to heal my husband? Or—death! Why couldn't God have "taken" him one of the times he overdosed on drugs? Wouldn't that have been easier for him? for me? and—oh, God—for those precious boys? What about them? "Dear God," I prayed, "Why did it have to come to this?"

I cried and I cried and I cried. I screamed at God! I begged and pleaded with Him to do something. "Oh God, please help me!" I prayed again and again.

And He did help me. He tenderly quieted my sobs. Who else but God could do that? In my worst moments, I realized His love for me—His wondrous love! He reminded me often of my precious boys, outside playing in the yard, and their need for me to be strong. He gave me needed strength that evening to pull myself up from my chair and prepare our evening meal. There was peace in our house that night because God was there with us.

The boys and I lived alone for seven years. There were many struggles and never enough money, but there was always an abundance of love. I kept my faith in God. He was my source for life. I took the children to church and taught them of God's love in our home with daily devotions. That has made the most lasting impact on their lives.

In 1970 I remarried. God gave me a wonderful husband and stepson. It was not easy, merging the two families; but as always, God was there and His love meshed and molded us into one happy family.

I hope I never forget, never need to be reminded that God is always there—in all of life's struggles. He truly lives "inside" us, when we believe that Jesus Christ is His Son and are willing to accept Him as our Savior. This is God's promise! We can be confident that God is always there! He gives us our new beginnings!

Fran Jones Snyder lives in Taylors, South Carolina with her husband Earl. She is a member of Taylors First Baptist Church, a Sunday School teacher and choir member. She is a member of Mo-Med, a Mobil-Medical Mission team made up of doctors, dentists, nurses and by people who spend two weeks each year in the back country of Brazil working with the poverty-stricken people. She is a volunteer teacher for the Laubach Literacy Association and does some volunteer work for the Boys' Home of the South, with boys from broken homes. Her husband Earl is on the board of directors. She has four sons—Jim, Michael, Barry, and stepson Eddie.

10
My Struggle with Fear and Depression
by JANET SPROUSE

I felt I had finally arrived. I had a challenging job teaching nutrition to low-income homemakers in the mountains of upper East Tennessee. This was my dream come true. I was really helping people. I had financial security for the first time in my life. I had a cozy apartment that seemed to welcome me home after a hard day at work. I had friends. I was involved in an active, caring church. I was, at twenty-three, ready to take on the world.

But something happened for which I was totally unprepared. As if overnight, and without warning, my life began to turn dark and dismal. I told myself I did not deserve all the good things that were happening to me. The low self-esteem I had had as a child and adolescent, for what seemed to me no reason, plunged even lower. I began to feel pressured and threatened, but I could not identify why. Having such a range of negative feelings about myself was terrifying. I felt as though I were in a box, struggling to come up for air, only to find the lid being nailed slowly shut.

Speaking before groups was an integral part of my job. I had been fully aware of this before I accepted this position. While I had always experienced stage fright before speaking in public, my reactions began to be extreme. I would feel as if I would rather die than face the audience. My fears were reflected in my voice. The soft voice that had been mine was replaced by one that was broken and forced. I desperately needed a way out of my "box," but I did not know how to begin to remove the nails.

I remained in a state of constant prayer as I asked for God to help me in this or that situation. I begged and pleaded for God's help. I read every Scripture passage on fear and committed them all to memory. I listened intently to every sermon, believing that one day I would "happen" onto the answer. It would fall out of the heavens as the manna had fallen to the Children of Israel in the wilderness. After all, I certainly felt that if anyone had ever wandered into the wilderness, it was I.

When my answer did not come quickly and miraculously, I despaired. My voice worsened. The effort to speak took every ounce of strength within my being. The words came out choked and broken. I sounded as if I were crying even when I was speaking in a normal conversation. My agony was greatly intensified when persons would ask me what was wrong with me. I had no answer for them, just as I had no answer for myself. Talking on the telephone was a disaster. Every time the phone rang, I felt like running away. The normal daily routine became a burden for me as I struggled through ordering food at a restaurant, through calling for doctors' appointments, and through something as simple as answering the doorbell. I could take nothing for granted. Everything I did had to be meticulously planned in order to avoid embarrassment.

What I had at first felt was a case of stage fright had turned into a way of life for me. The pervasiveness of my problem was so complete that every aspect of my life was affected. When I planned a nutrition lesson, I increasingly involved my audience in order to remove some of the pressure from myself. I became adept at avoiding certain situations. At the office when the phone rang, I would "conveniently" be out of reach so that someone else would have to answer it. My subtle forms of evasion troubled me greatly. My turmoil took another turn as I recognized my deceptions. I repeatedly asked God for forgiveness.

There were always those terrifying circumstances that I could not avoid. One year I had to do a canning demonstration at the county fair. A radio reporter came up and thrust a microphone to my mouth. Before I knew what was happening, he was asking questions. My throat felt paralyzed as I forced out the words. Afterward I felt as though I was worthless. Life held no joy for me. I could not even answer a few questions I knew thoroughly.

I began to suspect that everyone noticed my voice. I dreaded having to speak at all. My search for the answer continued. I began to read books on depression, worry, and nervousness. I devoured these books as I sought help. How I wished to read about someone in similar circumstances, but I never did. I felt different. Nobody in this world had ever had a problem like mine, I told myself. I felt utterly, completely alone. Why was this happening to me? Why? Why? Why?

Had God deserted me? I began to question my faith, but I still went to church and taught Sunday School. In a crackling voice, I would attempt to teach a group of teenage girls. As we came together each Sunday morning, my problems seemed to diminish in the face of their concerns. To my surprise, not one girl ever questioned me as to why I spoke the way I did. They encouraged me with their humor, their honest questions, and their love.

Although this feeling of desperation never fully left me, there were instances in my work when I was able to help people in spite of my problem. I discovered that listening to other's problems and concerns was a privilege. To my relief, people in need did not hear my broken voice as I sought to help them. Their greater need was for someone to reach out to them.

New possibilities were unfolding in my personal life. I met a young man who was to change my life. For the first time, someone cared about my hopes, dreams, and fears. My voice problems persisted, but here was someone who accepted me just as I was. Having my husband, Larry, by my side meant that I was no longer alone.

We became even more involved in our church, especially with the youth. I still avoided certain situations, but I was able to push myself to coach a girls' softball team and to help Larry with youth activities. Instead of retreating, being with Larry helped give me courage to forge ahead.

Larry shared with me his calling into full-time ministry. In order to prepare himself for his calling, he felt led to enter seminary. So we both quit our jobs and moved to Louisville, Kentucky, where Larry entered The Southern Baptist Theological Seminary. We had no jobs and no friends there.

Once again I felt overwhelmed. I became deeply depressed, and my voice reflected my depression. I had to get a job, but where? I drove to one of the shopping malls to start filling out applications in the stores there. I sat in the car and prayed and prayed that God would help me just ask for an application. As I walked up to the receptionist, I wondered if I would be able to get the words out. The agony of forcing myself to speak was almost unbearable. My job search eventually led to the Seminary Child Care Center. The position open was for an infant teacher. The thoughts of being a primary caregiver to babies frightened me. I knew nothing about babies, but I accepted the job and found that the language of love comes in many ways, not just in words. A smile, a hug, a kiss, or an empty lap are all ways to communicate love to a child. I found that I needed them as much as they needed me. The joys the infants brought me enhanced both my life and my husband's life.

Something else happened. Through my increasing awareness of child development, I began to wonder if the reason for my problem with my voice was somehow connected to my childhood. Maybe something in my childhood was missing. My curiosity led me to books about children, but I still had no concrete evidence to support my theory.

In Larry's last year of seminary, my depression deepened. I doubted my self-worth so much that I began to think of suicide. During this time, I found myself wanting to hide from people. I did not want to be with people or have to talk to them. I wore two faces. The face I wore to our weekend church was one of lightheartedness. By the time the weekend was over, I would be physically exhausted. My other face was how I really felt. I was troubled to the very depths of my soul. I was in pain, a pain that sears the heart and wounds the spirit. Larry patiently listened over and over again to my agony. He and I were both confused about how to release me from my bondage.

During Larry's last semester, he took a course in Human Crisis taught by Dr. Andy Lester. This course sparked Larry's interest in human suffering. Indirectly, I was affected also. Larry wrote a paper on death in that course. When he brought home books about death and dying, he encouraged me to read them. I found it very difficult to do this because they made me remember my mother's death when I was seventeen. I discovered that I had not dealt with my grief adequately. In fact, the resurgence of these feelings only plunged me deeper into despair.

I was alone in the apartment one day. I picked up a book and started to read aloud. Even alone, I could not get the words to come out. I hated myself. *I should kill myself,* I thought, but Something stopped me. Out of this intense confrontation with myself came the feeling that help lay outside myself. I had tried to answer all my problems, and I just could not do it.

Larry served as my mouthpiece as we searched for the person to help me. We were led to a very kind and caring woman. With her, I was able to recount past hurts, past memories from my childhood. This woman served as a role model for me as she showed me that a woman can be a wife, a mother, and a career person. She also served as a bridge to lead me to a patient and gentle therapist when we moved to a new city.

The decision to undergo therapy is very difficult. I often felt a push to confront my problems that was paradoxically accompanied by a pull to remain the same. This constant push-pull tug on the emotions creates within the person undergoing therapy a perpetual state of disharmony. While I was never comfortable with myself the way I was, the prospect of changing the "old me" was very frightening. My push for continued growth has been the desire to live the rest of my life learning how to deal with my fears and depression.

After Larry and I moved to our new church home, I once again experienced a deep depression. My fears about not living up to the church members' expectations caused my self-esteem to plummet. Every week in therapy I discussed these fears. Gradually, I came to realize that the ideal standards I expected myself to attain were self-imposed.

I began to seek fulfillment in directions in addition to our church work. I did not know how to start. What did I really want to do with my life? I was certain that I wanted to help others in some way. How to do this was a mystery. Over and over again in therapy I expressed the desire to fulfill this need within me. My voice problems complicated the situation. While I could feel this push to go on, I also felt a pull to not venture out. What if I failed? Maybe I was mistaken about this urge within myself. My greatest fear was that nothing lay inside my being that could really help anyone else.

With much encouragement from Larry and from my therapist, I hesitantly decided to try. My starting point was to talk with a career counselor. Once again, Larry paved the way for me by making the appointment. In this counselor, I found a competent person who understood my needs. The work we did together brought to light my skills. She opened the door to new possibilities for me. Somehow I caught her enthusiasm and certainty about my being able to find my niche.

The end result pointed to my working in a helping profession. As I reviewed my life, I began to remember how I learned to listen as a teacher and what satisfaction I enjoyed from helping people. Could it be that the books I had read on suffering were somehow a start of my preparation for a career? My life began to take on purpose and meaning. Maybe my pilgrimage had not been in vain.

My next obstacle was my reluctance to return to school. After my four years of college and our three years of seminary, I felt the last thing I wanted was more school. However, I could not deny the direction my life was taking. More education seemed to be the key to unlock the door. I just was not sure I could walk through that door.

I prayed about it, talked about it, and thought about it constantly. I was still afraid that I could not succeed. I asked Larry to pick up a catalog and an application for me. Just holding the catalog in my hands caused me much anxiety. I filled out the application, mailed it, and told myself that I could always back out. After all, I probably would not be accepted anyway.

I was accepted! Immediately I began to think about what area I wanted to study. My interests pointed to education, and, to my delight, counseling was an area within education. The entire procedure of discovering this direction seemed so ironic. I was having to do things I did not feel ready to do. How could I put myself through going back to school when I had so much trouble doing anything completely alone?

With my schedule completed and confirmed, the months before the first day of class had dwindled to days. My anxiety was almost unbearable. My throat felt paralyzed. Here it was, the first day of class was to begin, and I was not ready. That Monday was a frigid January day. The cold I felt, however, was from a chill within. I drove to the campus not knowing if I could even go into the building. I stepped out of the car on rubbery legs and walked to class. I was the first to arrive. Others started coming in, and they all seemed so matter-of-fact about being there. They were chatting and laughing, and I was miserable. Finally, the professor arrived and announced that the class had been cancelled due to the weather. I almost ran out of the building! I had been reprieved!

A day later, I faced the same situation as my second class was to start. I wanted to give up. Should I even try? Larry encouraged me to just drive to the campus to see how I felt when I got there. So I did. I walked to the building and went in. People were hurriedly going to class. I turned the corner, took one look inside the classroom, and turned to leave. I walked back to the door. I felt overwhelmed by fear. *I cannot do this,* I told myself. I left the campus that night never expecting to return.

I had failed. My tears did not relieve the pain. There were no answers for me. As I turned this experience over and over in my mind, I had a thought. If Larry would go with me, maybe we could explain my situation to my adviser. I felt a peacefulness after this decision had been made.

Much to my surprise and delight, this professor was wonderfully understanding and helpful. He was willing to accept me into his class knowing that I would probably be unable to participate in class discussions. He also talked to my other professor who was equally understanding and helpful. I was elated.

I continued to doubt if I could do the work. Tests and papers had been a part of my distant past. Sometimes my hand shook so much that I could barely read my notes. As the classes progressed, my interest deepened. I was learning things that were relevant to life. I also learned truths relevant to my life. I became hopeful again and interested in other people. One day in therapy, we were discussing my newly gained knowledge when my therapist said God had ordained for me to be in those classes. I knew it was true. God had guided me to those professors in order to learn more about myself.

I saw these professors as my "helpers." They were facilitating my growth. They accepted me as I was. They had competently shared their knowledge in such a way that learning became exciting. Other "helpers" God had provided along my pilgrimage started to come into my focus. God had not deserted me. He had been with me that day in the apartment when I first contemplated suicide. He had brought Larry and me together. He had placed people along my way who had helped me during my darkest days. Finally, God had made me realize that it is OK to need others. While God has not removed my pain quickly, He has guided me through my journey even through my darkest moments.

At this point, my voice is improved but not completely normal.

I still have many fears, and I am still dealing with my childhood. The difference in me is that I am able to live in spite of my pain. In fact, my pain has given me a reason to live. My pilgrimage has helped to create a close marriage bond for Larry and me. My hurts have enabled me to really feel another's suffering. My search for answers has helped me to recognize God's presence and assurance. Recognition of my "helpers" has encouraged me to be a "helper."

Now I am more independent. No longer do I rely on Larry to pave the way for me. Becoming the person God intended me to be has been and will continue to be the most significant challenge of my life. I know now that growth is slow and difficult, but growth is the only way to remove the nails that had tightly fastened the lid of my "box."

Janet Sprouse is a graduate student in education at Lynchburg College, Lynchburg, Virginia. She enjoys writing, crafts, and the outdoors. Her husband, Larry, is the pastor of Hunting Creek Baptist Church, Big Island, Virgina.

11
Breast Cancer

by JUDY HAMILTON

When I heard those words, I panicked: I was lying in the recovery room after having a breast biopsy, and I listened as the surgeon told me it was a "bad tumor." I cried and felt like I was going to be sick. At the same time, I kept repeating: "I didn't want it to be this way." I felt that in a very short time, I would die.

Just three months earlier, I had watched my mother lapse into a coma and die of liver cancer. Before that, there had been several other losses of family and friends. Death had been such a frequent visitor. I felt it would soon happen to me, too.

It wasn't as though I was terribly afraid of death. I just wasn't ready yet. I had been a Christian since childhood, and I knew that someday I would live eternally with God. But I had a husband and two children whom I loved very much, and I didn't want to leave them. I wanted to see my children happily married, and be here to love my grandchildren, if God so blessed us.

The next time I awoke, I was in outpatient surgery where I saw my husband, Fred, and our minister, Lloyd Hamblin, waiting for me. Fred's first words to me were "Talk to me, don't shut me out." Those words didn't really sink into my mind at first because I was numb. Gradually, I would find out just what he had meant.

I went home after a little while, still in a panic, not really able to comprehend what would happen to me two days later. I felt like running away someplace where no one could find me and pretending that nothing was wrong. My good friend from church, Ruth Sole, called to ask if she could come to see me that afternoon. While she was there, she didn't try to tell me all the answers to my problems. She just simply said, "Trust in the Lord." Before too long I was able to pray, and by evening I felt I had come to grips with the situation. The Lord had come through, and I began to have a peace in my heart. I spent the next day grocery shopping, withdrawing from a college class, and making arrangements to be away from home for a week.

I decided to make a special effort to share my thoughts, fears, and joys with Fred as much as possible without causing him too much extra anxiety. I knew this is what he had meant by "not shutting him out." He would support me and be with me all the way. Of this I was sure. His love for me was demonstrated in so many ways each day. I knew it would not change just because I was going to be a little different physically. But, even so, I began at that time to think about reconstructive surgery, perhaps at some later time. At least I knew it would probably be an option.

This was the first big hurdle I had to face. Once I was able to say, "I have cancer, I will have a mastectomy, and life will go on for as long as the Lord wills," I felt I had come a long way. Perhaps it may not happen in one day with you, as it did with me, but it will happen if you put all your faith in God.

Please don't think I was not ever afraid after that. I was. When I went into the hospital for the surgery, there were many times when I said to my Lord: "I'm scared; please take away my fear and give me peace." I was amazed at how quickly He answered my prayers and I could relax.

The surgery went smoothly and without much discomfort. My husband and children were great. My son, Mike, eighteen, and his girlfriend, Judy, and my daughter, Kristi, fourteen, visited me often. I could feel their deep concern and possibly a little fear of the future. My brother, Jim Backus, and my sister, Virginia Woody, and their families were also there giving me encouragement and love. I knew my niece, Pam Atkinson, and her family in another city were praying for me, as well as my brothers and sisters in Christ. I could feel the power of those prayers.

Before I left the hospital, I was told I should have at least one year of preventive-type chemotherapy, since the cancer had spread into one lymph gland. I didn't look forward to this, but since I had been with my mother as she also was given chemotherapy for a year, I wasn't too afraid. She seemed to get along pretty well, managing to work part-time as a foster grandmother at St. Joseph's Hospital. Unfortunately, her cancer had spread too far and the chemotherapy only served to lessen her pain.

No matter how "together" you and I think we are, there will still be times of anxiety. One of those periods of time for me was when I began my first treatment. I was very nauseated and afraid it would be this way every time. It was hard to even drink a glass of iced tea. The taste of the chemicals was very plain, and I couldn't eat at all. When I finally gave in, about two days after the beginning of the treatment, and went to the doctor, he offered to admit me into the hospital where I could be given nausea shots around the clock for the remainder of the treatment that month. It seems that the first treatment was pretty hard for my body to adjust to. Since I was upset and nervous, I was quite willing to go. After a few more days, I seemed to be able to tolerate it better, and I was back home in a week. After this one beginning treatment, I didn't have to go back into the hospital again.

During the week, I realized what a source of strength I had in Christian family and friends. I knew how much my husband, children, and close family members cared, but I was overwhelmed at the loving concern of my friends. It meant so much to have a hug from Sally, Judy, or from Barb, our minister's wife, or to have a prayer offered by Lloyd, or our assistant pastor, David Dye. I will always be so grateful for all of the visits of church family and of volunteers in the hospital with whom I had worked and had grown close.

I found there are many good things that can come from bad circumstances. One of those for me was getting to know my brother better. He was an employee of the hospital where I was and became a daily visitor. Also, my sister-in-law, Peggy, was to become a very good friend and someone on whom I could depend.

The first treatment began a time of testing and trials, but also a time of learning to cope and new joys. I kept busy with family and church activities and tried to make life as normal as possible, even though a lot of the time I'm sure I was not easy to live with. Cards and notes in the mail from friends always gave me such a lift. Summer was not far away, and I looked forward to being outside in God's beautiful world and going on a vacation to the ocean.

I soon learned what it was like to have a really close friend to share with. Sally Radabaugh has been that person to me by always being there when I needed her. She spent many hours sitting with me in doctor's offices and cheering me up. I hope I can be that kind of friend to whomever I am led to by God.

Surely the trials and hard times that are placed in our lives are there for a purpose. For me, I believe that the purpose was to prepare me to have compassion and empathy with those in similar situations and to be used by God to help them.

Don't be surprised if along with the second treatment you begin to lose your hair. This, to me, was one of the hardest things to which I had ever had to adjust. Eventually, I lost almost all of my hair. I felt so frustrated and angry I didn't know if I would ever be able to be happy again. My daughter, Kristi, found me one day sitting on the floor of our family room, crying very hard. When she put her arms around me and asked what was wrong, I told her I didn't want to lose my hair. I will never forget her wise and loving answer to me: "Mom, it doesn't matter, you're still the same person on the inside." As I'm writing this today, I feel the tears coming because I love this caring teenager so much for helping me to see what is really important.

Fred helped me to pick out my first wig and made me feel I was still attractive. Several times he took days off from his job to be with me for doctor's appointments or just to spend the day with me.

Our son, Mike, was so good about running errands for me and buying groceries when I didn't feel like going. It just seemed the whole family worked together to help make things easier for me, and I appreciated it so much. During those months we did many family things that we had not taken time for previously. I'm not trying to say that it was easy, but it could have been a lot worse. We seemed to learn to appreciate each other more than before.

It is very easy for you to imagine problems where there are none, when you have once experienced a serious illness. It seems as though every ache or pain must surely be the beginning of another malignancy. After five or six months of treatments, I found myself in a deep depression. One day I was particularly upset and fearful. Because of my weakened condition and some aches and pains, I had convinced myself again that I was going to die. It seemed that all I could do was cry. I was so tired. I didn't really feel like doing anything that I knew I should be doing in my home.

I tried to pray, but I couldn't decide if God was really hearing me. But the Bible says in Romans 8:26 that the Holy Spirit prays for us when we are unable to make our feelings known to God. Without a doubt this was a time when the Holy Spirit interceded for me. When I was at my lowest, the Lord Jesus gave me the assurance I needed. He didn't stand in front of me so that I could see Him, but just whispered to me: "You are not going to die—trust Me." He said this twice, and I knew without any doubt that He had revealed Himself to me in just the way I had needed. From that moment on, whenever I doubted, I would think back to that day and remember His words of comfort.

I have always loved to go swimming in the summer, but because of my hair loss, I didn't feel comfortable going to a public pool. I'm sure this was vanity on my part, and I should have tried to overcome it. But because my brother and sister-in-law had built a pool in their yard, I very often went there to swim. Peggy made me feel so welcome and at home. This was an enjoyable time.

Short trips by myself or with Kristi also helped. We would go to visit my niece, Pam, in Ohio, or go to Charleston to see a good friend, Thelma. Many times I would just go to town for lunch with my sister, Virginia, or to her house for a visit. I always came away cheered up. I thank God for all of these wonderful, caring people. Since I lived in my hometown, I had a lot of family and friends close by. But if you live in an area new to you, a very good way to make friends is through church activities. I think you'll find that most churches will be warm and friendly and will make you feel right at home.

In September, I started working three mornings a week in a preschool at a church in our community. Seeing fifteen four- and five-year-old children learn and play together is a real thrill to me. This has given me just enough to do to keep me from worrying so much about my problems, and I still have time to do things at home and church. God provides the things we *need* at just the right time. I have always loved my mother- and father-in-law; but after losing both my father and mother, I needed and appreciated them even more.

After my eighth treatment, and after having several infections of various kinds, I began feeling my body had taken all it could stand (of course, if necessary, I would go on to finish). One morning when I got up, I began to pray about what I should do. After some advice from a couple of people, and talking with my husband, we went to talk with the doctor. When I asked him if he would consider having my tests and scans run early, and let me stop if all was well, he agreed. I felt a peace from God about doing this, and as it turned out, I was able to stop after nine months.

I had my final treatment in December, and it is now four months later. It seemed that the chemicals would never leave my system and let my hair grow back and let me regain my strength. Even now, almost five months later, my white blood count is still below normal. But my hair has grown in even thicker than before; I have more energy; and best of all, the nausea is gone. During the last year I gained some weight, which happens to some people during treatments. I am slowly beginning to lose a little of it now.

If you are taking treatments, and feel the time will never end, believe me, it will be over and you will look back to discover you have forgotten a lot of the suffering that you are presently going through. You might ask, as I have, "What if it happens again?" This is a possibility we have to learn to live with. My doctor explained that he could not give me any guarantees; only God could do that. God guarantees us in 2 Corinthians 4:8-10 that even though we are pressed on every side by troubles, we will be safe if we live in Christ. This, and many other passages in the Bible, have given me strength and hope for the future. I just have to be faithful in my prayer life and study of God's Word and put my trust in Him.

Judy Hamilton and her husband, Fred, have two children, Mike, nineteen, and Kristi, fifteen. They live in Washington, West Virginia. Judy works as an assistant teacher in a Methodist church preschool program. She plans to undergo reconstructive surgery on her right side. She has decided to have a simple mastectomy on the left side (a preventive measure) and to follow with reconstruction.

12
The Empty Nest
by ELIZABETH PUCKETT

At the foot of the steps, I pause and take a deep breath. *Wait, there'll be plenty of time for this later.* I think, *No, better do it now and get it over with.* I go on upstairs to my son Wayne's room, bracing for the pain of the emptiness I will find there. It is real. Wayne no longer lives here. The bed sags where he slept, but his pillow is gone. The "pep" banner the cheerleaders made for him still hangs in its place. His sports trophies still sit on his dresser. His stereo is gone. Scattered here and there are mementos of his teen years to be kept and treasured, left behind as our son packed for college. Tears have come easily since we left him at the campus yesterday. Wayne also struggled for composure as we said awkward good-byes. Now the tears spring to our red-rimmed eyes with every thought of him. We are a close family, and it was like being torn apart to leave him there.

Now, as I survey his room, I cry for my firstborn baby, for the loving toddler, for the brave little boy entering kindergarten, for the energetic young preteen, and for the teenager who was never rebellious, though he often questioned our rules. I cry tears of sorrow for our loss of him to adulthood, and tears of joy for the person he has become.

For a while, I sit on his bed and reflect on the changes that have come in my life as I prepared for this time of letting go. There has been much turbulence this spring and summer. Of all the changes in my life, this has been the toughest time.

Lloyd and I had been married five and a half years when

Wayne was born. Doctors had told me I would be unable to have children. I was devastated because I had wanted a baby so much. I didn't think about how short a time they are babies, about raising a teenager, and certainly not about letting them go when they grew up. I just wanted a baby. I thought all my dreams would come true and all my needs be met if I had a baby. When I was told I couldn't have children, my desire for a baby intensified.

After trying for three years, I was finally able to become pregnant. My happiness was boundless when our son was born. When I held Wayne, it was as though I was complete, and I had a reason for being for the first time. When we brought him home, we laid him in his bassinet and stood gazing at him with such awe, joy, and contentment. We felt that he was the most beautiful, most perfect baby, the most exquisite of all jewels. Lloyd and I grew much closer to one another in our new role as parents.

Three years later, we had another baby, a little girl. She was just as perfect, beautiful, and wonderful as Wayne. Because we thought we couldn't have children, we saw both Wayne and Toni as miracles. We never lost the wonder of receiving these gifts from God. We have felt strongly our responsibility to raise them in the way they should go. We endeavored to teach them Christian values, to be upright, and we tried to help them reach their potential. They have been the joy of our lives.

I worked a while after Wayne was born, then chose to be a stay-at-home mother. We were fortunate that Lloyd's income was sufficient to live on. My time and efforts during the day were centered around the children and the home. We had a small farm and I did a lot of the work, but I was always at home with them. As preschoolers they were a full-time job, but as they got older, they did not require so much of my time; nor did they place so much stress on the house. But I was still very much needed and kept busy all the time.

During my years at home, my contacts with the outside world were limited. The longer I was away from people, the more I withdrew into myself and my family and the more I struggled with my self-image. Finally, I didn't have anyone who was my friend who was not in some way my friend through Lloyd. Even in the church, I was Lloyd's wife, not just myself. I was being what I thought everyone wanted me to be. I tried so hard to please everyone (and pleased no one) that I lost who I was. No wonder I stayed at home where there was only Lloyd, Wayne, and Toni to please. As I cut myself off from support and encouragement from other sources, I came to expect too much from my family.

Now, suddenly it seemed, the children were almost grown. Out of nowhere, I was confronted with change in my most important relationships. First, Wayne was leaving for college, with Toni not far behind. While dealing with this, I realized that my marriage was deteriorating, mutually taken for granted. Finally, I realized that I had no goals of my own.

Looking back, I can see that all we had done in relation to the children was focused on aiming them for adulthood, trying to build solid character in them, enabling them to make the right choices. The reason for each of these was that they were growing up. Yet that was a remote thing, like old age—you really don't think it will happen to you and your children. After all, this son of ours had spent almost all his time for eighteen years in our home. How could he possibly be ready to leave us?

Wayne, our miracle son, this enormous presence in our lives, would be absent from our home. His creaks up the stairs would not be heard anymore, for our football player is the only one heavy enough to make them sound that way. Our grocery bill and the laundry would be drastically reduced. The change in our lives would be instant and dramatic. Wayne would not live here full-time again. We wanted him to be normal, to grow up, to grow away from us because this was as it should be—but not so soon. This is my world that is changing, and it hurts.

Wayne had been the one I could turn to for understanding my feelings, my hurts, and my fears. I would be losing my confidant, my listening post. We have sat and talked for hours. He laughs and says that whenever he had a football game the next day and needed extra sleep, that was the time Mama would choose to come and talk an hour or more past his bedtime. I would miss my son and this house would probably echo without him. I wondered how I would be able to cope with it. He would return now and then, but it would not seem like "home" to him anymore. The emptiness wasn't my only concern; he was going away from me to a place where he knew no one, out of my reach, out of my control. Had I done my job well? Was he ready? If he wasn't, it was too late; I had run out of time. I'd done all I could do.

When Wayne and Toni were in their early teens, I felt that I had all the answers. Now I was afraid. What if my answers were wrong; what if I had created in these children of mine lack of confidence, just like I had had? Would they have more self-doubts than I had? They seemed to be well-balanced, fine people; but had I prepared them for life outside my home, my protection, my guidance? Had I given them so many answers that they could not stand alone? Had I made them depend on me to the extent that they could not depend on themselves, that they had no strength in themselves? Had they taken my faith, rather than developing their own? Were they good because they were afraid of our reaction? Did they feel that if they ever did anything wrong it would destroy our love for them? Did they believe that our love for them was conditional, that they must be perfect, must make good grades, must succeed in life?

I wanted to cling to this time when they were still at home, to go back and undo some of the mistakes I had made, to go back and savor some of the good times. Yet all I could do was record these memories as they grew toward adulthood and independence with the same eagerness that I did. Turning loose would be the hardest part of raising them. I hoped we could allow them their breaking away time without making them sever our relationship.

With Wayne's leaving for college, I was faced with the knowledge that in only three years, Toni would leave also. How quickly they have grown up. All my past roles were ending in some way. Panic rose within me. Everything I had been for eighteen years would be needed no more. It was vital at the time, but never again would they need my interest, my abilities, and my time to be centered around them. How would I adjust to an almost empty home? I had not considered or prepared for the time of leaving. I had been too busy keeping up with their changing needs. Now they needed for me to change. The commitment I had to my role as "Mama" had kept me going even when society said that to be "worthwhile," I had to have a career. It had been easy then to answer that my family was my career. Now who would I be when I had no one left to mother?

The most frightening aspect of all this was that Lloyd and I would be alone together again. Our marriage was not what everyone thought it was. Everyone, including our children, and even we ourselves thought we were the ideal couple. We put up a good front and got along OK. Now I discovered how shallow our relationship had become. How well would we get along without the children's companionship and our involvement in their activities? Perhaps we had allowed the children to become *too* important to us, and we had pushed communication with one another aside. We had come to take one another for granted, and we did not take the time to really be together anymore. Could we rebuild a closeness between us?

As I thought more and more about these things and struggled to find the answers for us, I became convinced that I needed to feel needed and must contribute something worthwhile with my time. I felt an urgency to find a role to fill when Toni left for college. Who would I be? What was I going to do? Must I leave the environment I loved and seek employment outside the home to be fulfilled? Could I be a whole person if I *just* stayed home? After devoting myself to my family, would I now be without purpose?

At Wayne's graduation, the speaker said that without setting goals, you didn't go anywhere. I realized that the only goals I'd had were goals someone else had set for me. I had helped others reach their goals, but had reached none of my own.

Seeing myself and my life in this new light caused me to despair. It seemed that all my roles were changing, and change is hard for me. I like the comfort and security of "life as usual." I knew it was in God's plan that the children grow up and away from us, but I wanted to hold on to them. I panicked for them and for myself whenever I thought of the future. This demanded that I take stock and seek some guidance. I prayed for help, but it seemed my prayers bounced off the ceiling. I felt far from God. Perhaps I blamed Him for my distress; but whatever the cause, I sure didn't feel any closeness to Him. I kept praying, though. Even when I felt it was useless, I just couldn't turn loose of that strand of hope. I also sought guidance from Lloyd and from a friend.

My friend Linda listened to my struggles and prayed for me. She proved herself to be on my side by her constant encouragement. Her confidence in me helped me to see my value as mother and wife, as well as my potential in relation to the world. She kept praying for me, even about things I considered insignificant.

Lloyd prayed for me sincerely too, though not everything was wonderful between us, and we went through some real trials before all this was resolved. I couldn't understand why I didn't have peace when I had tried so hard to live as a Christian. I was impatient and lost faith in prayer, but God was working through my anguish over my future without the children. He guided me and kept me on the right course, even though at the time I couldn't see His hand in it.

There was no one point when I saw that everything was working out, but gradually I was able to focus on a new direction that would fit in with my role as mother, wife, and self.

The first step toward finding my new role was to take some aptitude and interest tests at our local college. Surprised to find I possessed strengths I was unaware of, I was encouraged to pursue my own path. The tests opened my eyes to talents lying dormant within me and possibilities for exciting ventures available to me. With encouragement from the college adviser and from my family and Linda, and with guidance from the Lord, I've set some goals for myself in line with these new realizations. I've enrolled in our community college and plan to go on to the state university. I hope to earn my degree in some form of counseling or teaching. I am as excited about my new directions as I was as a teenager.

When I think, *Why, I'll be forty-seven by the time I graduate,* I realize I'll be forty-seven anyway—whether or not I go to college! I need this for myself, and I don't feel selfish in seeking it. By developing my own abilities, I will be a better wife, mother, friend, and especially a better Christian. It seems now that I am open to new opportunities. They are everywhere. I have developed an interest in writing, and I am finding this an exciting way to express myself.

I have realized that instead of being what everyone else wants me to be, I first have to please the Lord and myself. By trying to be everything to everyone, I have failed them and myself. No wonder I had lost my identity and floundered in self-doubt. I failed to be the unique individual God created me to be. It's funny to realize that all through the years, I've encouraged just that in Wayne and Toni, yet failed to do it myself!

Now, as things fall into place, seemingly of their own accord, I can see God's leading in it all. I see that I was miserable because I was allowing other people to control my life and set my goals, rather than allowing God to use my abilities in His own way. It is so reassuring to see in my own life that, though I fail Him and make terrible mistakes, He is still in control. He is working everything together for good because I am His. I know I will make it. I will become the very best "me" that I can because of the healing He has effected in me. He is showing me that I can do it, that He will help me, that He will open the doors.

The struggles are being resolved. I have a newfound peace about Wayne being away at college. I am confident that I can trust

God to care for him and that Wayne will show the results of being raised in a family who loved him, where he played a key role. We have done our job, and it is now time for him to take charge of his own life, with God's help.

Toni still has three years at home. I will not abandon her. I will be an even better Mama to her, my lighthearted, fun-time friend who laughs and helps me stay young.

All my changing during this time affected my relationship with Lloyd as well. I am more myself for perhaps the first time since we were teenagers. I've had internal storms raging because I had not been at peace with myself or with God. Lloyd has changed in response to my new confidence. With understanding and help from him, I am on my way to becoming all I can be. Our marriage has been renewed in a delightful way as we have talked and worked our way through our problems to true communication and love for one another. The prospect of our being alone again is now exciting rather than dreaded. Only the Lord could have brought about this wonderful new relationship we have now.

The Lord has truly changed my life. When I finally gave up trying to earn His love and that of everyone else, when running my life became so difficult that I had to surrender control to Him, He took my despair and turned it into wonder at all He has done in so short a time. Because of His answering the prayers of my husband, my friend, and myself, the storms within me are over. I will grow to reach my fullest potential. I'm not there yet, but I'm surely on my way.

Returning my thoughts to the present, I rise from the bed feeling better somehow—renewed by the promise the future holds, not only for myself, but for Wayne, Toni, and Lloyd as well. With new joy and energy, I begin my task by picking up a soiled, worn sneaker. Just an old shoe, yet so vividly Wayne's that I smile even as the fresh tears spring to my eyes.

ELIZABETH PUCKETT

Elizabeth Puckett is a homemaker and free-lance writer. She and her husband, Lloyd, have two children, Wayne, eighteen, and Toni, fifteen. They are members of First Baptist Church in Eden, North Carolina. She operates their small cattle farm and enjoys reading, traveling, and meeting interesting people.

She is currently enrolled in the college transfer program at Rockingham Community College and plans to go on to the University of North Carolina to complete a degree in psychology.

13
I Was a Battered Wife
by LINDA HARDESTY

As I read the Sunday morning headlines and the article that followed, the newsprint grew darker and larger. I could feel the pounding in my chest. Each successive beat of my heart seemed to inflate the words until they towered life-sized before me. A young mother was stabbed to death by her husband after an argument. She died in the front yard of their home.

As saddened as I was by this tragedy, I knew why I was reacting so emotionally. That Saturday, after a violent argument, I, too, had reached my breaking point. For the first time, I had consciously thought of murdering my husband. I even knew which knife I would use. It seemed my only escape from the insanity that swirled around me. That story in the paper represented a kind of journalistic *deja vu*. It wasn't my story, but I felt it was. I knew how close I had actually come to turning someone else's stomach as they sleepily nibbled their toast and coffee.

I cut the article out. Those words had shocked me back to reality and I wanted a tangible reminder of how desperate I had become. I was at the crossroads and I knew it. One path led to the same life I had. Two children, a home, security, someone to go places with, who would work around the house and take out the trash. The All-American Dream except that, behind closed doors, I was a battered wife. The other path was longer. It led to divorce. It was the unknown, and it frightened me, too. But that day, after years of uncertainty, the veil was lifted. I was beyond the lies, beyond any hope of another reconciliation, beyond love.

I had allowed myself to believe that even my hatred for him was a healthy sign because it meant that, at least, I had some emotional feeling. Now that, too, was gone. I don't know when it happened. One day I had just quit caring. I couldn't even hate him anymore. I wasn't sure if many of my friends suspected the ugly secret in our lives. I had tried to hide it. But I knew I wasn't camouflaging the sadness in my eyes. Eyes that long since had lost their softness and their innocence. They were now glazed with an emptiness that belied their twenty-five years.

I knew I had my answer. My unknown future had to be better than the fears I lived with from day to day. The fear that someday our arguments, which had progressed well beyond the spat stage, would erupt in the same violence that now screamed from the headlines. I feared that I was depriving my children of a chance for a healthy adult life by exposing them to what had become a way of life to us. I knew that children from homes where there is domestic violence or child abuse often become abusers themselves. That would not be my legacy to them.

After struggling with this decision for years, it seemed I could almost pinpoint the instant when all my doubts were washed away. I felt a sad relief. This determined person was a far cry from the timid young girl who walked into the marriage. Of one thing I was certain—I would never allow anyone to dominate or abuse me again.

There was not as much media attention given to battered wives in the seventies as there is now. Like a cancer patient who can't face the illness, though, I went through a period when I denied what was happening to me. The few cases of abuse I read about were poor Peyton Place-type characters from the wrong side of the tracks. The husbands would spend every paycheck on drinking and come home and "knock his old lady around." I wasn't being beaten every day like they were; and besides, each time he hit me, he always promised he would never do it again.

I had convinced myself that there were no alternatives. I needed to believe those promises. Like the gorilla at the zoo, who fascinated me so each time we visited, I imagined our moves and expressions mirrored each other. We lumbered back and forth, seemingly with the weight of the world on our shoulders, occasionally glancing with feigned interest at the world outside. But hidden in that great mountain of fur and flesh was the same terror I knew. We were both trapped. But I had built my own cage. I began allowing this sickness to infect my reality. The patterns of the arguments and beatings were set, and I had gradually let it become an acceptable characteristic of our marriage.

I knew the years of rationalization were changing me. I was becoming someone I didn't like very much. I had always been shy, but being with people became painful. I wouldn't answer the doorbell or return items to the store. When my husband would belittle me I didn't want to believe him. But as my outside contacts diminished, I drew inward, wrapping myself securely in a cocoon of real and imagined inadequacies.

Later, even when things had started to turn around for me, I was still taking medication for my nerves and for hives, and sometimes drinking a "well-balanced" lunch of Canadian club and water. There seemed to be two forces battling within me. One, with no self-confidence and convinced, over the years, that it had few redeeming values. The other was a vague memory of a more gentle soul who had been lost in the bitterness. It began fighting again for its life.

At the suggestion of a friend, I sought counseling. It was difficult for me to overcome the stigma that I was seeing a psychiatrist, but after a few weeks I looked forward to my visits. That process of verbally painting the canvas of my life made me realize that I could blame no one for the outcome of my situation. The responsibility for my life rested in my hands, and it always had. Why had I refused to accept it? The answers weren't simple. I had to go back to the beginning to find them.

Our courtship would have struck fear in the hearts of mothers everywhere. It was the classic health textbook example of the day. We began dating when I was sixteen. He was seventeen. We went to different schools, and since we were both desperate for a romantic attachment, we began going steady almost immediately.

Even though I had been an excellent student in high school and had some outside interests, no accomplishment seemed to boost my self-confidence. But that was all right because he had an overabundance—enough for both of us. I saw in him all the things I didn't have. He conversed easily with adults, while I was always complimented on being so quiet and "such a lady." I thought the two were synonymous.

He would take me to concerts and parks and movies and out to elegant dinners. He bought me roses and gifts too numerous to list. I was very flattered by the attentions of this young boy who could probably be dating anyone, but chose me.

I was secretly pleased when he would come out of his way after work to drive by my house and blow the horn at 2 AM. I never got very upset when he would show up after school to take me home even if I had made other plans. I suspected at times that he followed me, as he would appear coincidentally at places where he knew I would be. After graduation, when I lived on campus, he used to come into the courtyard and fling rocks at my dorm window just "so I would know he was there."

By October of that year, after three years of dating the same person, I realized how isolated I felt. I told him I wanted to break up. Two weeks later, I found out I was pregnant. He was ecstatic. I cried on my wedding day. I knew he was obsessed with me, but it was too late. He had me and we both knew it. Abortion was never mentioned. I didn't consider any other alternative and would not to this day accept raising my daughter on my own. (As I've grown older, the sanctity of life has become so precious to me. I can bear the memories of my troubled marriage. I could never bear having taken a life God gave.)

I set out to make the best of my situation. I began to drown myself in seeking perfection. My house was immaculate, cleaning was done every day, and heavy cleaning (what I now do once or twice a year) was done on Fridays. Washing and ironing I did on Mondays. I changed my baby's outfits several times a day and bathed her religiously. Any spare time was spent in sleeping, curling my hair, cooking, and watching television. We weren't going to concerts, and we couldn't afford elegant dinners. There were no more flowers.

The violence that marked my marriage began subtly. The first time I was seven months pregnant. After an argument he pushed me out the front door. I tripped down a few steps of our tiny second-floor apartment, just before he threw most of my clothes on top of me. I was shocked, but I knew he had been really angry. I dismissed the incident believing it would be the one and only time. It wasn't.

That was the beginning of a seven-year relationship that to an ardent television viewer would look like a rerun of last week's show. Oh, the reasons for our fights varied over the years: money, the children, our families, his job, my job, personal hygiene, drinking, friends. The main characters were always the same.

Afterward I would look back and try to analyze exactly what single incident caused our fights, but there never seemed to be a key. Nothing we could sit and talk about resolving or avoiding the next time. The arguments seemed insignificant compared with the outcome. It was almost as though we knew the ending to the episode, and it didn't matter how we got there.

Upon reflection, I don't think the things we argued about had anything to do with our fights. There was a rage growing inside my husband, something he couldn't deal with internally. If he didn't let it out, I think it would have consumed him. He was a time bomb ready to explode. Sometimes it was just easier to let him explode. His behavior after our fights became well rehearsed, too. He seemed to feel better, more relaxed somehow, but always remorseful.

The most puzzling reaction of all would be his tenderness. He would stroke me as though I were a wounded animal. If I repelled his touch, he would physically force my arms around him and make me hold him. Once, after he beat me with a belt, he brought the belt to me and begged me to beat him so he would know how I felt. I did once. I remember that feeling of causing someone else pain more than I remember all the beatings I suffered.

As our relationship deteriorated, I seemed to be losing touch with myself. I became as frightened of me after our fights as I was of him hitting me. When he would hit me I would put my arms across my face or try to crawl away if he knocked me down. Sometimes I would fight back. I felt I was going berserk. Many times, I would sit and chant incoherently like some black-robed mourner.

One Saturday afternoon, after being beaten, locked in the basement, and once again having my clothes thrown on top of me, I was able to phone the police. I was still overwrought as I tried to give them the report. I suspected they thought I was a madwoman. My husband walked calmly into the room and asked what the trouble was. He said I had been acting like this all day and that he would try and calm me down. He seemed so much in control; maybe I was crazy, as he insisted.

I didn't think much about God in those days. That was before I knew God takes us when we're broken, when we can't sink any lower. Oh, I prayed the Lord's Prayer at night, and I loved the Twenty-Third Psalm. But I had an image that God wanted squeaky-clean Christians fresh from the baptismal pool. He certainly didn't need a problem child like me. I now know that I was not forgotten. Even when we are too weak to have any faith left, He remains faithful to us and will help us (2 Tim. 2:13). Maybe He heard me when I cried out "Oh, God! Oh, God!" as I crawled on my stomach to get away from the blows. I know I prayed the day I hid for eight hours under a mattress in our basement closet as I begged not to be found.

Like an object in a swirling hydraulic of white water, I was caught in the swell of a marriage that was pulling me under. But I popped back out, and I did not, could not, have done it alone. I was like the skeptic who saw only one set of footprints in the sand during days of despair and assumed that the Lord had forsaken him. When he questioned God, God replied that the one set of prints were His—that he had carried the one who felt deserted.

I know God carried me during the really hard times. He walked next to me when he thought I could handle the problem. And He showed me the path. There were too many doors that were opened at the end of my marriage for me to consider anything else. Fate would not have been as generous.

About two years before my divorce, a friend told me of a temporary position as a legal secretary. I laughed at first. My business experience consisted of a ninth-grade typing course and two years as a customer representative for the telephone company. Despite my fears, I called and was hired for two weeks to replace a vacationing secretary. What I lacked in skills, I decided to make up for in being conscientious and friendly. At the end of the two weeks, my employer called me in. The other secretary was quitting. He wanted me to replace her permanently. He would train me and later agreed to pay for my education while I earned my paralegal certificate. One day a housewife, the next a legal secretary! I knew it probably wouldn't have made the New Testament, but it was the option I so desperately needed.

Being in a new environment was wonderful. I made new friends, took on more responsibilities at work, lost weight, and started feeling better about myself. I seemed to be able to draw on some untapped resource to give me courage to change our situation. I realized he was never going to change, so I had to.

I began trying to interrupt the patterns that we had set over the years. When I could feel a fight coming on, I would gather the children and go visiting. I was no longer interested in defending myself or retaliating when he verbally abused me. When he said I was "fat, ugly, and stupid," I would agree. When even that didn't work and he blacked my eye, I told my friends and our families what had happened. I was no longer protecting him as

I had in the past. I made sure my doctor had a record of my bruises and the cause of them.

As our financial situation improved and I became more independent, I was unknowingly nailing his coffin shut. Our relationship existed on his dominance of me. Once I removed that power from him, he became frightened. He needed me much more than I needed him. As I talked of divorce, he seemed determined to show me we should stay together for the children and our families. When those attempts failed, he preyed on my sympathy.

His lying and drinking became worse. He was shoplifting everything from meats to fingernail files. He would become very morose and pretend to take large quantities of pills in various suicide attempts. After one incident, my mother came to pick up my daughter and me. As she was pulling out of the driveway, my husband ran behind the car and fell on the ground to make us believe he had been run over.

The saddest time I remember was the day he sat in our basement with a shotgun on his lap threatening to kill himself. I had pleaded with him in the past not to do this. I would take the gun and assure him I loved him and that we would work it out. That day I was tired of the games and the manipulation. I went downstairs and begged him to shoot himself or me. I couldn't bear the anguish of this bizarre union anymore.

I look back on those years in much the same way you might, as a person reading the details of someone else's life. My ex-husband once said he remembers the good times we had. I know there must have been good times. I don't think about them any more than I think about being a battered wife, ten years ago.

I am remarried now. I have since learned that two people can argue without verbally slicing each other into pieces. But there are a few faint scars left from the past. We are careful not to say hurtful things in the heat of an argument that even "I'm sorry" can't erase later. Sometimes, when the situation gets too tense, I have to leave the room. Not because I'm running out on the discussion, but because something inside me won't let me stay.

I have asked my husband not to put his arms around me when I'm angry because I feel so suffocated. We talk about the fact that sometimes I react negatively out of a memory in my past.

Mostly, I am aware of the positive changes in me. I once read that out of the most crushing setbacks, one often develops a dignity of intention. I am not advocating domestic abuse as a way to build a "quiet growth in grace and character" (Heb. 12:11, TLB). But I am more patient, less demanding of myself and others, and more compassionate. If I feel that someone is overreacting to a situation, I try to understand that there may be something in his past coming back to the surface. My children are my most precious possessions. I have discovered the power of a smile. I am having a love affair with nature. My senses can now absorb all the joys that my suffering obscured.

I have accepted my share of the responsibility for the marriage and its failure. I have never regretted my decision. Husbands and wives don't have the right to hit one another. There should be a mutual understanding that the first time, if there is a first time, must be the last time. There are two conditions necessary in domestic violence: the abuser and the one willing to be abused. My concern is for the latter.

I found my answer to the question all battered wives need to ask themselves: "Why do I let him beat me?" I thought I deserved it. I felt guilty about the circumstances of our marriage. I knew we were both a disappointment to our parents. I had committed a sin, and this was my punishment. I was too ashamed to ask for God's help. I figured He was probably disappointed, too. But the Bible tells me in Jeremiah 8:4-5: "When a person falls, he jumps up again; when he is on the wrong road and discovers his mistake, he goes back to the fork where he made the wrong turn" (TLB).

God loves you and me. He gave us a choice, and He doesn't expect perfection. He asks only that you and I strip off anything that slows us down or holds us back, and especially those sins that wrap themselves so tightly around our feet and trip us up.

Let us run with patience the particular race that God has set before us (Heb. 12:1).

I'm still in training for Him, and we talk every day now.

Linda Hardesty and her husband, Michael, live in Columbus, Ohio. She is the mother of three children: Kristy, eighteen, Jason, fourteen, and Erica, nine. She enjoys playing tennis, going on walks, cooking, and art.

14
My Spiritual Crisis
by SUSAN COPPOCK

The crisis that happened to me in the fall of 1984 was one among several that has happened over the course of my life. Everyone must have a good half-dozen over the span of a lifetime, I think. But I have picked this one because it was so different from all the others. The others came from without—my parents' illnesses and deaths, the termination of relationships (male and female), moving, the struggle to get an education and become an independent person. This crisis was spiritual, and it took place within me.

I became aware that someone or something was trying to get my attention. I realized that for weeks I had been walking around trying to do my ordinary daily tasks and having an extraordinarily hard time doing them. I would be driving the car and my eyes would fill up with tears. I would be reading and realize that I had read and reread the same sentences again and again without understanding. And always I was conscious that someone or something was trying to tell me something. But who and what?

Perhaps you're thinking—aha, a breakdown. Here we have a nice middle-class white bread lady, married, the mother of three, with no job outside the home and lots of time to focus on herself and her state of unfulfillment. But you would be wrong, or at least presumptuous, to think so. My life is full, and I am happier than at any time in my life. This was as true in the fall as it is now. I have known people (both male and female) who were going through emotional breakdowns. I have seen the signs, and I knew that this was not the case with me.

So, then, what could this crisis be about, I kept wondering. Then I began paying attention to my thoughts, and I began to find some clues. I realized that my appearance is very important to me—maybe part of my self-image involves looking nice, being made up—"putting on a face to meet the faces that you meet." And what would happen to my self-image if I were no longer pretty or made-up or young? But I didn't want to think about this, so I moved on to the next clue.

I began to hear myself talking—I mean hear the meaning behind the words. I have always prided myself on being verbal and smart. I can hold my own verbally in almost any gathering, and an evening isn't complete if I can't make everyone laugh at least once or zing out a few one-liners that make a few jaws drop. So, this is bad, you ask? Maybe just a little mean-spirited, I reply. Because someone has to be the butt of the joke. If I'm going to be "on top," somebody else has to be "on the bottom." Or what's even more subtle, I can be the butt of the joke too. The joker and the jokee at the same time. What a miserable thing to do to others and myself.

I began to realize that I arrange my life so that I win all the time. I choose, I test new limits, I rationalize, I forgive. I am the center. The last line to a Christmas poem called "The Miraculous Birth" by Joyce Carol Oates says, "The miraculous birth is your own." I have thought many times of how intoxicated most of us are with ourselves—with our births, our thoughts, our words, our accomplishments, our sense of power.

So now you may be thinking, if not a breakdown then liberal guilt. Gobs of literal guilt with a strong dose of female masochism added—a twentieth-century cocktail. But "no" again. I am conscious of the danger of blaming myself unnecessarily.

After squirming around trying to avoid recognizing these clues, I realized that whoever was trying to get my attention was not going to go away. And I could not run away. So I stopped and found I was looking at myself, the real me who lives inside, the one who knows that the mascara and the humor are trivial—fun, but trivial. I saw myself with no illusions, and I was afraid.

I know that God spoke to me. He wanted me to get a good look at myself and my values and reevaluate the direction of my life. What is so ironic is that I have always been afraid of being superficial. When I was a child, it was enough, if you were a girl, to be pretty and malleable. To be made into a beautiful ornament by a man—your father, then your husband—was the natural order of things. This always seemed shallow and mean to me (it still does), and I have spent most of my life trying to overcome this early and destructive conditioning. God shook me and said: "Look at what you have become. Look at the nonsense you are concerned with. Look at your wasted potential. Where is the person I always meant for you to be?" I can't begin to express how deeply hurt I felt by this very accurate criticism.

I heard a minister talk recently about God knowing his name and how terrifying that knowledge is. I agree. For as long as only I knew my name I felt in control, I could be on top, I could direct the whole of my life—maybe sometimes badly, but I could live with the consequences of my mistakes because that's what grown-ups do, isn't it? But for God to know my name, to pick me out, to want me and my life, that terrified me. It still does, and surely always will.

I do not understand any of this very well, but I have had a few insights that might be helpful to you, if you are experiencing these same feelings. One is that it is impossible to be on a spiritual journey without being painfully aware of how flawed we are. Whatever flaw is most painful is exactly the area to work on.

Something else I know is that beyond the flaws is the center of me, where God is. Getting to the God in me is my life's real work. It is a daily struggle. While I am struggling, I am sometimes aware of you and your struggle, and when I help you there God is in that encounter, too. So God is in the present as well as the future, and this understanding is the spiritual encouragement that I need to continue the struggle and not give up.

One thing I have begun to do is to pray. I realize that I cannot make it to the end of my life without help—even the help of friends isn't enough. I have to know, as I do now, that God is carrying me along, that there is an "undercurrent of joy" in my life. I have finally accepted myself because God has accepted me and has forgiven me. I have discovered, with great relief, that my arrogance is not so great that I can refuse the hand that He offered me.

So what makes me so special, you might be asking? Nothing. Nothing and everything. I am not more special than you are. The point is, you and I are all special. He knows the number of hairs on all of our heads, only some of us know that and some of us don't. And what does He want us to do with our specialness? Believe, live a good life, be kind and compassionate, help those less fortunate, live out the simple truths that are so hard. Be an authentic person.

Susan Coppock and her husband, Michael, have three daughters: Emily, Laurel, and Selena. They live in Weston, Massachusetts. Susan was educated at the Institut Heubi, Lausanne, Switzerland, and the University of Massachusetts. She graduated in 1974 with a B.A. in Political Science and English. She enjoys writing, bird watching, and cooking.

15
My Grandmother's Death
by DENISE GEORGE

On a hot, sticky August afternoon, I sat in the porch swing, my body heavily laden with child, grieving deeply the death of my grandmother. I felt sad, alone, and angry at God. The past few months had been spent in dreaded anticipation of "Mama's" death. And now it had happened. At eighty-two years of age, her body was tired. My mother's words over the telephone a few hours earlier still echoed in my ears: "Denise, Mama is in heaven now."

"Why, God?" was my first reaction. "Why couldn't you have let Mama live just a few days longer? Why did you take her now?" I demanded to know. My Heavenly Father, who had been so near to me in times past, now seemed distant and indifferent.

Within ten days, my second child would be born by Caesarean section. How I feared the surgery. The date had been scheduled. A sonogram had shown that the unborn child would be a daughter. We had named her Alyce after my grandmother. I had prayed so hard that Mama would live to see her, her own little namesake. And now, only ten days had separated Mama from her new great-granddaughter, Alyce. I could only shake my head, shed more tears, and demand angrily, "Why, God?"

I continued to rock in the porch swing, feeling sore at God, as I watched my two-year-old son, Christian, at play in the yard. I had already attended to the rituals of the early morning following her death. Calls had had to be made, the car packed, funeral flowers ordered. Ordering the flowers proved difficult for me.

Mama had so loved flowers. I had painstakingly chosen a pale lavender flower arrangement. In the center, I had placed a single pink rosebud surrounded by baby's breath. Mama would have understood the pink rosebud, I thought, a remembrance from her unborn namesake.

The funeral would be tomorrow, Sunday, after church services. Some three hundred miles away, the whole family would be together at my grandparents' home, grieving in Mama's death but also rejoicing in her life. They would all be together while I sat here at home, swollen and suffering from the heat, ready to deliver a baby, with only a toddler to comfort me. At my grandfather's request, my husband, Timothy, had left an hour before, making his way to Chattanooga to bring the funeral message. I had so wanted to go with Timothy, but with the birth close at hand, the risk to the unborn child seemed too great.

Suddenly, Christian's sharp scream interrupted my thoughts. "Christian!" I called as I searched the yard. There, in a corner of the yard, my eyes rested on a small heap of little boy sitting in the grass, crying and holding both knees. Tears dropped from his chin as he tried to explain how he had tripped and fallen and skinned both knees. I picked him up off the ground and sat him on the porch swing while I went into the kitchen for a bandage and medicine. After the scrapes had been cleansed and bandaged, I wrapped my arms around his small frame and whispered in his ear: "It'll be all right, honey." A few moments later, Christian leaped from the porch swing and bolted back to his play.

How often Mama had used those encouraging words—"It'll be all right"—to comfort me when I hurt. I had heard them so often, they just seemed to roll naturally off my tongue whenever someone needed to be reassured. Mama had been my comforter, a loving and kind grandmother, who had very early taken me under her wing and had told me of Jesus' love. My spiritual guide, she seemed to always have the right answers for whatever problem I faced. Her reassuring "It'll be all rights" nurtured me through the frequent scrapes of childhood, the problems of teenage years, the decisions of dating and marriage, and the anxiety of new parenthood. How very much I needed her strength now to help me face Caesarean childbirth. *What would I do,* I wondered, *without Mama's wisdom and counsel to carry me over the rough spots of my life?*

"Why, Lord?" I asked again and again. "I do not understand your ways, Lord. You have so long been my Comforter. Where are you now, Lord? Why must I endure this pain alone?"

I felt the strong swift kick of little Alyce, who lay nestled within me, so eagerly awaiting her advent. Mama had so wanted to live to cuddle this new great-grandchild, her only namesake. A month before, during our last visit together, lying in bed and almost too ill to sit up, Mama had slowly risen to her feet, walked to her dresser drawer, pulled out a folded ten-dollar bill, and placed it in my hand. "This is for my little namesake's birth day," she had instructed me. "Please buy her something real nice from me."

As I sat thinking about the two Alyces, both of whom were so very dear to me, who in this life would never meet, I felt the tears once again fall down my cheeks. Death in the midst of new life. I wondered how I could concentrate on the life brimming inside of me when I was so overcome by the death all around me.

For most of the morning, I rocked in the porch swing, staring straight ahead into a garden of wilting flowers, but seeing nothing. My lovely grandmother was dead. I was grieving all alone, feeling separated from God. The intense August heat made me feel sick. My body was so heavy, so swollen. I was miserable, with no one to offer me comfort.

Wallowing in self-pity, so worried about my own condition, I suddenly became aware of a tug at my sleeve. "Mommy? Mommy? What's wrong, Mommy?" Christian demanded to know. Looking down, I saw a tiny face surrounded by a mop of tousled blond hair and big blue eyes that stared in puzzlement at my tears.

"Mommy's sad today, honey, because Mama has died," I tried

to explain to one I thought too young to understand or to grant sympathy. But, to my surprise, with all the love and concern a two-year-old could muster, Christian put his arms around me and hugged me. Then bringing his face close to mine, he whispered the comforting words he had heard me so often whisper to him. "It'll be all right, Mommy."

As if hearing a voice from the past, so wrapped in tender love and understanding, my grandmother's well-worn expression took on new meaning. Somehow I knew it would be "all right." I could only smile as I watched Christian return to his backyard play. "Yes, Christian," I whispered to myself. "It'll be all right for sure."

The very words I needed to hear, the concern and sympathy for which I longed, the gentle touch that brought me back to reality had come from a little child. At that moment, I realized that I had not been forsaken by my Heavenly Father, my Comforter. For He had been by my side all along in the presence of my small son. God was with me even in my anger toward Him. He sought to comfort me even when I questioned his ways.

Death in the midst of life. It no longer seemed as confusing to me anymore. For in death as in life, God is always close by. The Great Comforter would be beside me, comforting me, in the death of my grandmother and in the birth of my daughter. "It really will be all right," I told myself out loud. I had to get on with my life, for I had a two-year-old to feed that evening and, in ten days, a baby to birth.

I sat in the porch swing rocking gently for the rest of the afternoon, thinking of Mama and thanking God for the gift of comfort He had sent to me in the form of a little child.

Denise George is a free-lance writer and author of five books. Denise and her husband, Timothy, a professor at The Southern Baptist Theological Seminary, and their two preschoolers, Christian and Alyce, live in Louisville, Kentucky.

16
Blind Prejudice
by HELEN PARKER

Even though I was born blind, my first and most cherished ambition was to become a teacher. As a child at play, I often pretended to be one. Whenever anybody inquired, "What are you going to do when you grow up?" my answer was always the same. "I'm going to be a teacher."

During my freshman year at college, I began teaching a Sunday School class of high school girls at my home church. The joy I derived from teaching them renewed my determination to pursue the career I had chosen. By then, I had definitely decided to become a high school English teacher.

Everyone who knew me, including my faculty adviser at Centre College, agreed I had made the right decision. It never occurred to any of us that my blindness might prevent me from attaining my goal. Hence, no one bothered to look into the matter until my senior year at college, the year I was ready to do my practice teaching.

Needless to say, the information that a blind person could not obtain a teacher's certificate in Kentucky, the state where I lived, was quite a blow to all of us, but especially to me. (Fortunately, that is no longer the case.)

My first reaction was anger, followed by self-pity, then doubt. I wanted to lash out at God for allowing my well-laid plans to go awry, at society for its discrimination against the handicapped, and at myself for the resentment and self-pity that were building up inside of me.

"It isn't fair," I kept lamenting. "I've passed all the required courses except practice teaching with above average grades. I know I can teach. I've been teaching a Sunday School class of high school girls for over three years, and everyone says I've done a good job. My pupils love and respect me. Isn't that proof I can teach?"

As always, Mom tried to comfort me. "Honey, I know how disappointed you are," she soothed. "But many times, like it or not, life is unfair."

She reminded me how disappointed Moses must have been when God did not permit him to enter the promised land, and how David's hopes of building the Temple were dashed. I suppose she chose Moses and David as examples because they were two of my favorite Old Testament characters. "Maybe," she suggested, "you should stop fretting about a door which has been closed and should start asking God to guide you to another career. You know He never closes one door without opening another."

"But Mom," I protested, "I've always dreamed of becoming a teacher. Besides, you know how limited job opportunities are for the handicapped. Even if I wanted another career, which I don't, what else can I do?"

"I don't know," she admitted, "but I'm sure there are other things you can do. That's why I suggested you pray about it."

"I'm much too upset to pray about anything," I fumed. I still felt as if God had let me down, regardless of what Mom had said.

"That's why you need to pray," she answered. "Just tell God how you feel. He'll understand." Then she added: "A verse of Scripture that helps me when I don't know how to pray is 1 Peter 5:7: 'Casting all your care upon him; for he careth for you.'"

For a moment neither of us spoke. Then Mom asked: "Have you forgotten the help you received in answer to our prayers when you wanted to attend college?"

I hadn't forgotten. How could I ever forget? As upset as I was, I remembered how impossible the idea of a college education had seemed when we first discussed it. There had been so many obstacles to overcome: the country was in the midst of the worst depression in history, my parents couldn't afford to send me to college, student loans and college textbooks for the blind were not available at that time. And, to aggravate matters, if I attended college, someone would have to read my assignments to me.

The events of the summer following my graduation from high school flashed through my mind. One by one each obstacle that blocked my path had been removed. In June, Centre College, a school within commuting distance of my home, had granted me a scholarship. Shortly thereafter, a government agency had agreed to finance the remainder of my expenses. Next, a friend had put me in touch with a needy student who, for her room and board, was willing to read to me. Before the summer was over, I had managed to locate a good second-hand portable typewriter, and I had received enough money for graduation to purchase it. In August, my sister, Berta, had obtained employment within a few blocks of Centre, thus providing my reader and me a ride to and from school each day.

(Just recently I related those events to two members of my Sunday School class who were contemplating dropping out of school. After hearing my story, they decided to continue their education. The preceding Sunday, the mother of one of them took me aside and thanked me for the encouragement I had given her daughter.)

Even though I felt resentful that I could not become a teacher, my conversation with my mother and my reflections on past experiences made me feel less so. I promised Mom I'd try to keep my faith in God and in myself.

Casting my cares upon Him was easier than I had thought it might be. At first, I simply poured out my grievances to Him. Gradually, however, my prayers became less fussy. Soon I was beseeching God to help me find my own special niche in life and to give me the wisdom, strength, and courage to accept it. Knowing that my parents and other Christian friends were praying as fervently as I was reassuring.

It was not too long afterward that I decided to apply for work as a Braille proofreader at the American Printing House for the Blind, the largest publishing house of its kind in the world. (The printing house is in Louisville adjacent to the Kentucky School for the Blind, where I had received my elementary and high school education.)

On the day I mailed a letter of application and my resumé, I felt like my old self for the first time in weeks. The possibility of working in Louisville was exciting. My sister, Daisy, and several good friends lived there.

In an interview shortly thereafter, Mr. Ellis, the superintendent of the printing house, promised me the first opening. Since I still had a semester of college to complete, I found the waiting not too difficult.

I began my work as a proofreader in 1937, a position I held until my retirement in 1979.

As heartbreaking as it was to relinquish my dream of becoming a teacher, I learned some truths I feel worth remembering. I discovered that God's answer to prayers is not always yes. Sometimes it is no or wait. Sometimes we receive a better answer than the one we request or expect. That happened to me. As a proofreader of textbooks, I probably helped more visually handicapped students obtain an education than I would have helped had I become a teacher. Undoubtedly, the wide variety of material I had to read enabled me to become a better writer, a hobby of mine. My writing eventually turned into a second career.

I also discovered that God answers prayer in various ways. Sometimes He opens a door we mistakenly assume He has closed. That also happened to me. I believe God led me to a church where I have had an opportunity to attain my goal of becoming a teacher. For the past thirty-five years, I have taught an adult Sunday School class at the church I now attend. Although I was denied the opportunity of helping train young people to make a living, I believe I have had the privilege of helping to equip adults to make a life.

HELEN PARKER

Helen Parker, a gifted writer, speaker, and teacher, is the author of *Light On a Dark Trail*, Broadman Press, 1983. She has published articles in numerous denominational magazines. Mrs. Parker is married and is a member of Clifton Baptist Church in Louisville, Kentucky.

17
My Husband's Murder
by LORRAINE KAUFMAN

In the late sixties and early seventies, I was the wife of a medical doctor and a mother rearing four children. Those were turbulent years for our country. There was the Viet Nam War and the assassination of President Kennedy. Much unrest was in our cities. People were seeking equal rights. My home city, Louisville, Kentucky, was no exception. Even our children felt the tide of doubts and fears when we had an enforced curfew due to rioting after a Derby Parade. Our middle son's band had marched in the parade. The very nature of man called for courage to take arms if necessary for self-defense and property rights. Already my husband, Max, carried a gun in his car for protection, and we kept one at home.

We were a typical suburban family. I spent several hours a week in the car chauffeuring the children to band practice, piano lessons, and swim practice. All were excellent swimmers, so we made two trips to the pool daily in the summertime.

One day nothing seemed to go right. We had stopped for hamburgers on the last trip home. It was a Wednesday, and Max would not be home. As we drove away from the restaurant, my car door flew open. Going through the subdivision, a child in a car backed across our path. Safely home at last, Max Jr., oldest and son number one, showed us his graduation gift from my brother—a New Testament in a brand-new paraphrased version. As we read this fresh new edition of God's Word, we became very excited about how real and alive the words seemed to be. This was the hope that I had prayed for to create a closer walk with my Lord. In times past, I had felt that God was far away. I had felt forsaken. I knew now that there must be more fulfillment in God's plan for my life than being a wife and a mother.

Looking back, I can see how God was preparing me for the dark hours that lay ahead that night. That evening at church I shared these treasured words with my friends. I was overjoyed with thankfulness, a mountaintop experience. It was the first day of July, 1970.

It was about 9:30 PM when I returned home from prayer meeting. Son number two, Stan, had just hung up the telephone. He said that his daddy would check the emergency room, and, if nothing was there, he would be home shortly. Stan was fifteen years old and very dependable to take messages. Peter was ill, and Nancy, the apple of her father's eye, and our only girl, seven, had gone to bed.

By the time I talked with Stan and Max Jr. about the prayer service and folded the clothes, it was 11 o'clock. I read my Bible and turned out the light at 11:30, thinking I would stay awake as I usually did. But I had a certain peace and thankfulness which must have lulled me to sleep.

I was awakened at 1:30 AM by the telephone. A woman's voice on the other end asked if I were Mrs. Max Ervin. I told her I was. Then she told me she was calling from the General Hospital. She said that Dr. Ervin had been in a serious accident and was in a critical condition. She asked me if I could come down there right away. I was told to come to the emergency entrance, with which I was very familiar from Max's medical school days. I knew also that it was the best hospital because it was the university's teaching hospital, for which I was thankful. But immediately all the other aspects of the hospital flashed through my mind: the foul odors, dirty hallways, and the scores of people who sat in the halls waiting to see a doctor.

A sudden heaviness in my chest came upon me as though I had been hit by a baseball. I answered: "Yes, I will come right now."

As I hung up the telephone, my only thoughts were, "God, he can't talk. He didn't make the call. Oh my God, I pray that he is still alive. God, I will not think of anything except that he will be alive." I did not know how to pray.

I don't remember dressing. It was almost as if an invisible hand were guiding me to get my car keys and driver's license. Then, as an afterthought, I awakened Max Jr. and told him what had happened. My last words to him were, "We can only hope that he is alive."

On the way to the hospital, I talked and cautioned myself to stay in the proper lanes of traffic and drive slowly, repeating to myself to be sure to park in the emergency section and take my keys, as the nurse had told me.

When I arrived at the hospital, I went to the waiting room in the back that had been designated. I checked in with the nurse at the desk. The darkness of the room and the dirty floors and furniture all cast a gloom of uncertainty and hopelessness.

Shortly, two men appeared in street clothing, no doctor. My hope was gone. They were the coroner and detective. The coroner explained that Max had been shot twice, under the left arm and on the right side of the neck. It was sudden death. He never had a chance to live. I asked if I could see him. They gave me his wallet and twenty-five cents, and said it would be too traumatic for me to see him. I explained that I only wanted to be sure that it was Max. They explained again that it would not help me but only make me feel worse. Then the detective asked me about my husband. Did he have a girl friend? Did he eat dinner with a certain doctor? They were all negative answers. The coroner then asked me if I wanted to call my pastor and some other people, which I did. Afterward I returned home alone, mystified. But I felt God was in me, and I did not feel too frightened. My first thoughts were *How will I tell the children?* and *Shall I awaken them?*

The three boys met at the back door. They knew the answer when they saw my face. Still, I had to tell them their father was gone. The hardest fact to accept was knowing that a person shot him with the intent for him to die immediately, just the same as the man who shot President Kennedy, with the .22 gun in the same places of the body. The children were as stunned as I was. Not knowing what else to do, we went upstairs to the guest bedroom, and we all climbed into the old four-poster bed to try to rest until morning.

Soon we heard a car in the driveway, then another, and we rushed downstairs. Two couples, our closest friends, were at the back door. We sat down at the kitchen table and tried to put the pieces together as to why. A thief trying to steal drugs seemed to be the most logical motive, or, perhaps, anger at the lack of money on the victim.

Still in shock, I asked the two doctor friends if they would go to the morgue and view the body to be sure that it was Max. I needed reassuring. I kept hoping that there was some mistake. I found that truth is very difficult to face. It was never easy, and each time I was faced with the fact, it still seemed unreal. Max and I had never taken life lightly. We lived it one day at a time. As an anesthesiologist his patients were in a constant life-death situation during surgery. I was grateful we had made preparations for this very day by making wills and trust agreements for our children.

Events fell into place as a drama would onstage. Perhaps this was a reassurance that it actually was happening.

God only knows all who prayed, sustaining me that night and the days ahead. I felt lifted up by the Holy Spirit. There was no need for medication. The children and I put complete faith and trust in Christ. Two weeks later, I was told by a friend that the nurse at the hospital that night knew my husband and I to be Christians. She remarked that I had reacted to the news in a Christian manner. The Word of God continued to give me grace and hope in the church as my mother and grandfather had taught me it would.

The hurt of death was greater than I had ever anticipated. I was overwhelmed with physical weakness and emptiness of heart. A part of me had been removed. This must be death. Death to the part of me that was gone, and death to the one who had been a part of me, complete separation. I often thought, *Why did this happen to me?* Then the Scriptures began to come to me as I searched my Bible daily. One familiar simple verse I had taught young children in Sunday School was Psalm 56:3: "What time I am afraid, I will trust in thee." Also Psalm 55:22: "Cast your burden on the Lord, and He will sustain you; He will never permit the righteous to be moved" (RSV) and Isaiah 43:2: "When you pass through the waters I will be with you; and through the rivers, they shall not overwhelm you" (RSV). And, lastly, one of my mother's favorite verses, Philippians 4:13: "I can do all things through Christ which strengtheneth me."

The best consolation friends gave me, and seemingly the favorite, was "It takes time." Memories and nightmares often were relived when persons inquired harmlessly about Max's death. It was like opening an old wound anew, with all the pain, anguish, and uncertainty of an unsolved murder. Because of public scrutiny, I knew what people thought and were saying even though they did not say it to me. I set the facts I knew straight with our sons. They needed proper knowledge if they ever heard any unusual talk. During a period of four years, I never became quite at ease to discuss his death. Therefore I withdrew from police investigations. Through the guidance of the Holy Spirit, I wisely determined that my children were top priority now that Max was gone. My most earnest prayer was, "Please, Lord, grant me sanity for these days ahead."

Sometime in that first month, I received a book by Catherine Marshall, *To Live Again*. I had been clinging to Max's protective spirit for me and our family. We had never been separated for more than three times in twenty-one years of marriage. In the book I read that I had to turn loose of him, to let him go, in order for us both to be free, so that he could be at rest and I could go on with my life alone. This was what Catherine Marshall called a relinquishment. I discovered that this was a part of the healing process. There would be more loneliness. On the other hand, it provided me with a sense of relief. Only the spirit of Christ could heal. Through my tears and hope there was more to life than this.

One night, while I was lying in bed, I had a vivid dream, as if it were in real life. Jesus stood at the foot of my bed and said: "I'll hold your hand each night as you go to sleep." My husband and I had always held hands while going to sleep. I almost asked myself, "How did Jesus know?" This remained with me indefinitely as an everlasting token of comfort.

A new me was emerging from my cocoon. I changed my hair color and bought new clothes. I no longer wanted to be called Mrs. Ervin. I had forgotten that I had another name besides Mother and Honey. I took off my wedding band and regretfully destroyed all our love letters.

My feelings were two-fold. On one hand, I felt hate, guilt, and resentment toward my dead husband. On the other hand, my feelings were directed toward the murderer. The question often arose, "Did my husband ask for it?" Nothing I thought about made sense. Therefore, I leaned heavily upon God's mercy for my irrational judgment, in forgiveness, and for his cleansing power. I had to learn, as the apostle Paul said, to be content in whatever state I found myself.

Soon, decisions about the boys' schools, house payments, and my social life became a major part of my thinking. The two older boys went away to school, as their father and I had previously planned. Since I could not afford the house payments, it seemed best to sell the house we had built and move into a smaller one. My social life, and whether to date or not, was the most difficult decision. I definitely had to wait a year to date. I was not ready emotionally to share a new relationship; nor were the children. Looking back, I can see how my strong will accepted the statistics that there were more single women than men, and that most single men were divorced, as a guideline to date instead of patiently waiting for the Lord to provide the right person. I ignored the fact that God did provide the first time around in my first marriage, and He surely could do it again. All this I kept in the back of my mind, telling God: "I know what I need. I need companionship now." I did not like to go out with other single women. I felt uncomfortable. Still, I felt that marriage was several years ahead after the children were grown and had left home.

God did protect me while I dated, and I had more unhappy experiences. I discovered that God really did not want me to marry during this time. My four children were all I needed.

During these years, I had given up Sunday School leadership, but kept the class of Girls in Action of Woman's Missionary Union organization. My daughter, Nancy, was in this group. I became active in a Christian women's club. We were mostly lonely women, divorcées and widows, who felt out of place in the couples' society of our churches. Their testimonies of God's grace and forgiveness and beginning a new life appealed to me in a new way.

The singles ministry had not caught on in the smaller Southern Baptist churches. I felt like an odd number in my church. Out of these frustrations and feelings, I was able to be instrumental in organizing a singles Sunday School class. Hope had given fruit to courage and strength to reach out in a new ministry and meet my needs.

Each morning I began my day by reading four Psalms and one Proverb, from a paperback book published by the Billy Graham Associates. This paraphrase expressed the same anger and turbulence I felt, and then the peace and confidence that the psalmist had endured, as well as the praises for God's loving-kindness and mercy.

Some doctors' families looked down upon counseling. Our family had been no exception. Although I did not seek it, I read as many books on families in crisis as I could find. There were not many. I read one on relationships in the family that gave me some insights to my weaknesses and strengths in communicating to my children. I had almost never truly been a child in my first home. Girls did not climb trees or go skinny-dipping in the river. There was not much to do in a rural town in Kentucky. I envied my brothers every day of the year, to be free to do these activities. If I were only a boy. In widowhood I met the same disappointments—if only I were a man, I would be able to understand my sons better. Some books I read helped me to understand better the role of a good parent. I could not change overnight, but, at least, I understood why I thought a certain way and was able to make a few corrections in role playing of the parent, adult, and child.

By 1975 I decided to give up the historical "Able" house where we had moved in late 1970. Two of my sons were now married, and I had learned a new vocation as a medical assistant. I went to Ridgecrest with my daughter, niece, and sister-in-law. I made a firm commitment to Christ and His church. Nancy and I moved into a new condominium. Stan, my single son, was in the Navy. That year the Girls in Action class had a recognition service. Our church began a singles Sunday School class. New opportunities to witness were opening everywhere I went. I also became a part of an International Friendship Club sponsored by our associational Baptist women.

In September, our Girls in Action leadership decided to take the girls to visit a mission point of our inner-city missions. The purpose was to introduce our girls to the black inner-city girls, since preparation was begun by the local school board to bus children out of their school districts the next year to secure racial balance in the schools. That Sunday afternoon I met my future husband, Bill Kaufman, the Director of the Baptist Center in the medical area. He gave us a tour of the center. We had a grand experience but left hurriedly, as we had to attend evening services at our church.

Just as I started to open my car door, my conscience reminded me to return and give proper thanks to Bill Kaufman. Returning to thank him for the tour, I met him formally and gave him my name. He asked me if I were the widow of the Dr. Ervin who had been shot. I told him I was. This opened the door for him to share some of the tragedies he had experienced in his own pilgrimage.

Several years ago he had lost a youthful daughter in an auto accident, and recently his wife had died of a brain tumor.

In those few moments of sharing the intimate crises in our lives, the groundroots for a lasting relationship were laid. It's no coincidence to me that here was an answered prayer. If I remarried, I had hoped that my daughter, Nancy, could replace another's daughter lost in death.

We did not date seriously until the following January. Then, on April 3, 1976, we were married in my church at Hurstbourne, amid early blooming dogwood trees that lined the street.

I scarce can remember such happiness. We honeymooned in Atlanta and Florida. Then we attended a Christian Social Ministries conference in Stone Mountain, Georgia. Since Bill was affiliated with the Home Mission Board of the Southern Baptist Convention, I chose also to become appointed to work with him. I've never felt more belonging than I have as a home missionary. To be a foreign missionary had been a dream of my mother's. My late husband had often called me his "own special home missionary." He more than once had said I should have married a preacher.

At last, by the grace of God, I have found my call and my service—a pastor missionary's wife.

Lorraine Kaufman has become mission support chairman for Highland Baptist Church, Louisville, Kentucky, and leads prayer retreats and teaches mission study courses with her husband, Bill. Bill now works for the Kentucky Baptist Convention as State Brotherhood Director. Between them, they now have twelve grandchildren and one great-grandchild. Lorraine's daughter, Nancy, is engaged to be married this year.

(The person who murdered Lorraine's first husband, Dr. Max Ervin, has never been found, and the mystery as to why he was shot has not been solved.)

18
My Career Choice
KATHY FOGG BERRY

My four-cornered mortar board looked cute perched atop Micah's nine-month-old head. Impatiently pushing aside the swinging blue tassel, our son modeled my Southern Seminary graduation hat. Next, he grabbed my husband's graduation cap and impishly posed for his grandparents' camera. Graduation had finally arrived. The hard stuff was over; or was it just beginning?

It was a crisp May day in 1982 when Bill and I graduated from The Southern Baptist Theological Seminary. I held a Master of Education degree, and Bill, a Master of Divinity degree. At graduation, my aspirations to minister through writing seemed remote. We had diplomas, a son, Micah, and one job . . . for Bill.

Many choices confronted us during seminary: where to live, what to study, how many part-time jobs it would take to feed us, where to do field placements, how to sandwich field placements in between wage-earning jobs, and whether or not to start a family. How we could both fulfill our desire to minister and receive jobs in the same field, ministry, presented the most difficult decisions.

Many years earlier, at barely two weeks of age, I became acquainted with the cribs in the nursery of Monument Heights Baptist Church in Richmond, Virginia. Growing up in that church, I was nurtured and loved. Whether haltingly reciting a Scripture passage for an Acteens recognition service, or serving as associate pastor during youth week, I felt my church family's support. I loved the people in that church; but more importantly, I wanted to embrace the Christian faith they showed me.

Following my parents' dedicated examples, I felt the need for Christ in my life. At a young age, I accepted Christ as my Savior and Lord. Through the years, my relationship to Christ took on new dimensions. I felt God wanted my future in ministry for Him. Placing my life in His hands felt natural.

This relationship with Christ blossomed and faltered at times. While attending Bluefield College, located in an idyllic Virginia mountain valley, I became consumed with questions about how God wanted me to minister. Was I to teach, nurse, sing (I hoped not for my future audiences' sakes), write, construct buildings?

I had always loved to write. But at first I couldn't see how I could write and fulfill my desire to minister. Gradually, I felt convinced that expressing my faith through writing was right for me. Transferring from Bluefield College to Virginia Commonwealth University, I began to study journalism.

During college, my life and Bill Berry's life came together. Although we had dated off and on since high school, college years solidified our love. After college graduation, Bill left Richmond, our hometown, for New Mexico. He'd been appointed as a US-2er, a two-year post-college missionary in the United States.

I decided to work until January after our college graduation and then enter Southwestern Seminary to study religious journalism. Tentatively, Bill and I planned to marry after his two years in New Mexico were completed. We lasted two months apart. Getting married, we decided to attend seminary together, after US-2.

Finally, as seminary graduation approached, we joined other graduates in frantically writing and prayerfully mailing resumés. Bill sought a Christian social ministries position. I wanted a job writing or editing for a Baptist agency.

We were optimistic and unrealistic. Actually, there are only a few major cities in this country that could accommodate both of our ministry goals; but that didn't stop us from thinking we could both find fulfilling jobs. However, we gradually realized the complications involved as we both sought employment in the ministry.

This realization caused a lot of worry, self-searching, and crisis in our marriage. We constantly wondered: Should we both get a job? Would we go if just one person received a firm job offer somewhere? What if the job opportunity for one person was in a place the other person couldn't receive ministry fulfillment? How would we decide which person's job took precedence? Should one person's job be more important than the other's? And on and on and on we grappled.

Having a child born during seminary added to our questioning. Should one parent stay home with Micah? If so, for how long? Which parent? Did we want our child in day-care full-time? How would our working affect him? Would he be better off in day-care than at home with a parent who might feel unfulfilled career-wise?

We discussed these questions, and others, until every time we opened our mouths they were all we could talk about. Bill and I felt overwhelmed by questions we couldn't answer.

When the replies to our resumés began coming back, my nibbles were weak; Bill's were stronger. The Southern Baptist Home Mission Board approached us about serving in New York City. Bill would become pastor/director (a home missionary) of Graffiti Baptist Ministry on Manhattan's Lower East Side.

When Bill first mentioned moving to New York to me, I flatly responded, NO. I would not move to that notoriously dangerous and overactive city. But the second time the Home Mission Board called, they said, "Just look at the ministry position in New York. We'll fly you up there, no obligation to accept." They must have known us pretty well. Their persistence lowered my resistance. *What's the harm of looking,* I thought.

Arriving in New York City amidst the noise of taxis, subways, and millions of walking people, I felt overwhelmed. As we toured Manhattan's nontourist-attracting Lower East Side, the dire human needs of poverty, hunger, loneliness, homelessness, and violence stung me and began to melt my heart. These beautiful people living in New York need to know about God's grace and love. But who would go to such a place?

Surely God wouldn't call us to New York City. How could I work for a Baptist publication and live in New York City, a pioneer area for Southern Baptists?

Again, we went through the familiar barrage of questions. If we took the position, Bill and I wondered, would I feel complete or resentful? What did God want us to do? At first, we honestly didn't know.

Despite experience I'd gathered while working on a variety of secular and Baptist publications, no tempting job offers came my way. I began to take notice, though, of the free-lance writing opportunities which had come my way since beginning seminary. *Royal Service*, a Woman's Missionary Union publication, had asked me to prepare several articles. The Sunday School Board and the Southern Baptist Home Mission Board provided other free-lance opportunities.

I began to wonder if perhaps through free-lancing I could find my writing niche. Free-lancing, at least until Micah got older, could solve our career questions, I speculated. I could set my own schedule, choose which pieces I'd like to write, and enjoy a variety of assignments. As I continued to think of the free-lancing possibilities, I realized that by writing at home, I would have more time with Micah and time to minister through other channels.

I *could* fulfill my desire to minister through writing without a full-time position at a Baptist agency. In fact, as I became more excited with this realization, it dawned on me what a great place the mission field would be to write in and about. First-hand, I could write about what was happening to us in New York as God worked through us.

Bill and I continued to debate the New York move. There were many things to consider before accepting this position in such a "challenging" environment. The more we debated and discussed the pros and cons, the surer we felt that we should go. Once this decision was reached, a real inner peace washed over us. We moved to New York City in the hot summer of 1982.

Jointly appointed as home missionaries, Bill and I decided to share responsibilities at Graffiti. Bill used his strengths in social work, counseling, and leading Bible studies (among others). I worked with community women and girls. Because there were no other full-time staff members at Graffiti, we wore a lot of hats. We shared child-raising responsibilities, and I wrote while Micah attended child care several mornings a week.

Living in that city with its hustle and bustle provided constant writing ideas. The multitude of people, languages, foods, and cultures constantly stimulated us. Free-lance writing opportunities came in steadily, too.

While writing a Home Mission study book for the Home Mission Board, I was able to travel throughout the country doing interviews with missionaries about their ministry for Christ. This was exactly what I had always dreamed of doing! Living in New York, I'm sure, helped my free-lance career. Baptists wanted to hear about this unique city. This was a special time, enhanced by the birth of our daughter, Amber.

Despite all of these opportunities for writing that cropped up while we were living in New York, I occasionally longed to experience the permanence and professionalism of a full-time job. Somehow, free-lancing didn't afford those qualities. So, after we'd been in New York for two years, I began to feel inner conflict again. Bill, too, desired to utilize some skills lying dormant in New York.

At that point in our lives, 1984, the National Student Ministries Department of the Baptist Sunday School Board contacted Bill about becoming their missions consultant. He'd have the opportunity, in that job, to impact and involve thousands of students for missions. Living in Nashville, home of the Baptist Sunday School Board, would help my writing career, too. I'd have the opportunity to acquire work there or at one of the many other

Baptist agencies located in the Nashville area. After much prayer and deliberation, again we moved.

Working part-time at the Sunday School Board and maintaining free-lance contacts, I feel fulfilled. As conflicts arise, we've been able to juggle our career desires and continually reassess our goals. Although it has not been easy at times, I feel we've handled a lot of crises in our marriage by being flexible.

I'm often reminded of Isaiah 40:28-31, one of my favorite Scripture passages. God gives us the ability to walk on when we we feel too tired to walk. He provides strength when we're weary. God's leadership in our lives constantly challenges us and calls us to change when change is needed.

Bill and I feel a mutual commitment to each other's happiness. We want to grow as a couple as we help each other grow individually. Living together and cooperating together is not always easy, but it's always exciting!

Kathy Fogg Berry lives in Nashville, Tennessee, with husband Bill, son Micah, and daughter Amber. She finds fulfillment through writing for various publications, working part-time, and spending time with her family.

19
My Father's Suicide
by TERRY HELWIG

I survived the moves from ten states, seventeen towns, and twelve schools. I made it through three of my mother's divorces, helped raise my five younger sisters, and lost my mother before her forty-first birthday.

But none of that prepared me for the night the telephone rang in my Ohio home. The night I learned that my father had committed suicide.

The news, like a kick to the stomach, took me to my knees. Like a boulder, it tried to crush me. It magnified the pain of death, by what seemed to be a thousand times, because my dad did not have to die. He chose to. He chose to slam shut the book of his life. A life I loved very much.

How could that be? My father was a lamb of a man. A meek and gentle lamb. But somehow, somewhere, that meek and gentle man got lost.

I did not know he was lost. I knew he was having trouble sleeping. I knew he was worried about some things. I knew he was not totally happy. But I did not know he was capable of picking up a gun, pointing it to his head, and pulling the trigger.

Only three weeks earlier, my stepmother had called. "Your dad is really down," she said. "Why don't you talk to him. Maybe even try to convince him to come visit you. He says you're like a ray of sunshine."

So Dad got on the phone. No, he didn't think he could justify coming out.

"It's pretty expensive—even by bus. Why, I don't even know what we're going to do for fuel here on the farm next year—with inflation and all. Maybe buy a wood stove. Plenty of timber around here for that. I just don't know. Where's it all going to end, Terry?"

"I don't know, Dad. Why don't you come out and we'll talk about it? I'll pay your way. Please come for a while. It's been over a year."

"I know," he said. "I'll think about it. How about that?"

I hung up the phone never believing he would come. But the next morning he called and said he was leaving.

"And you're not paying for it either," he said as the receiver clicked in my ear.

I went to the grocery and bought his favorite foods—ham, bacon, potatoes, biscuits—if nothing else, we would eat well. I put clean sheets on his bed, rearranged my schedule as best I could, and waited.

When he climbed off the bus, he looked so tired. He did not usually look his fifty-odd years, but that day he did. I wanted to take him in my arms as I would a child and ask him what was wrong. I wanted to comfort him as he must have comforted me when I was a baby, although I did not remember many of my years with him.

I remember my mother saying: "When you're eighteen you can see your father or write to him if you want to. But not until then. I won't allow it."

So after my eighteenth birthday, I called him. The first time I saw him was at my wedding. I had known him only four years of my life. I cried walking down the aisle that day: My future husband was at the altar and my father was at my side.

From that day forward, I grew to love my second family—my father, his wife, and their daughter. Usually you love your father because you grew up with him. Well, my father was a stranger after all our years of separation.

But, oh, how I grew to love him, his gentle nature, his sensitivity. How I, too, could look out upon his moonlit fields and sense what he felt, the goodness and nearness of God. How I, too, treasured those walks in the timber, the night spent under the oak tree, our Saturday night bingo games.

That is why his coming meant so much to me. I wanted to help him feel better. I wanted him to know how important he had become in my life. I wanted to put all of my feelings into words. And I did.

We had a chance to say things that week that had never been said before. We read the Bible and prayed together. I remember sitting in the family room, our hands clasped tightly, while my father prayed a prayer more eloquent than any I have ever heard. So eloquent that my tears splashed onto his hand while he spoke. I felt so sure that things were going to work out for him. So sure that he was in God's hands.

He shared some of his fears with me. The ones about becoming older, more forgetful. The ones about his financial situation. The ones about his marriage of twenty-five years.

So many things were pressing in on him, so many doubts swirling in his mind. But at the time they did not seem insurmountable. That is why we talked about God, about the power of positive thinking, about how things were bound to get better.

I even remember one afternoon we talked about suicide. I will never forget what my dad said: "I hope I'm never crazy enough to do something that stupid."

I never realized it at the time, but I guess I took that statement to be some sort of promise. I must have. Why else would I have felt so betrayed when I found out he had killed himself? I felt angry. I felt hurt. He had as much as told me he would never do anything like that.

And if he really loved me, how could he have taken his own life? Did he have any idea what he was doing when he pulled the trigger? What made him "crazy enough to do something that stupid"?

I felt responsible. So responsible. If only I had said the right thing. If only I had tried harder, listened more. Said less. If only I had realized he was in such a state of despair. Maybe I could have helped. Maybe I could have saved him. Maybe . . .

It has been four years since that phone call.

In that time I have struggled with the "rightness" or "wrongness" of my father's actions. I have wondered where his soul is. Does he hurt anymore? Has he found the light at the end of his tunnel?

I still do not have the answers. No magic ointments. No cure. But I do have God.

Sometimes at night when my pillow is wet from crying, and I cry not so much for myself as I do for my father's action, it is then that I feel God's arms around me. It is then He assures me that His strength is my strength. It is then He reminds me that He is never any farther away than a prayer. And it is then He listens to a prayer of intercession for my father.

It is a prayer of mercy uttered long ago by His Son as he hung upon the cross. I have adapted it to my own special need: "Father, forgive him, for he knew not what he did."

Terry Helwig is a free-lance writer now living in Louisville, Kentucky with her husband, Jim, and their daughter, Mandy. She has published articles, short stories, and poetry in both the secular and Christian marketplace. Her book *Forgive Me, Lord, I Goofed!* will be soon released by Broadman. Terry says the moments she calls her own are spent within the pages of a book or in front of her typewriter. Some of her most pleasurable times: holding a sleeping child, petting a purring cat, and walking with God on a lonely beach.

20
My Crisis of Faith
by JO EDLIN

At first I was really disappointed; but after I left the surgery waiting room, my disappointment quickly turned to anger. This anger wasn't randomly placed on anything or on anybody. It was aimed directly at God. I felt that God had made a fool out of me and that He probably was enjoying a big laugh. Even through my tears and anger, I knew that couldn't be true. But how else could I explain what had happened?

Thomas was one of the sweetest five-year-old boys a person could know. His parents were committed Christians who definitely "practiced what they preached." One routine afternoon, Thomas and his mother were helping at the school paper drive. Just as they were loading the final papers, Thomas screamed and clutched his bleeding hand. His mother instinctively wrapped his hand in a towel and rushed him to the nearby emergency room. The steel door that Thomas had been closing had slammed on his hand and had cut off the tip of his finger. Thomas went through the ordeal of X-rays, exams, and endless waiting. When it finally came, the hand surgeon's verdict wasn't good. He masterfully stitched the fingertip back in place, but gave the parents only scarce hope for its healing. They were instructed to wait a week for the results.

During the wait, many prayers were offered for Thomas. His church family, which included me, prayed diligently for him. Our church had watched as God had directed lives, as He had healed marriages, and as He had restored health to diseased bodies. We anxiously waited for another miracle.

Almost a week passed. Wednesday night I experienced a strong urge to pray for Thomas. I enjoy my sleep and very few things awaken me. But the prompting was so real I couldn't sleep. As I prayed for Thomas and his family, I felt a flicker of faith to pray for the total healing of his finger. Gradually, I felt assured that this was God's will. I knew God could, and now I was becoming excited about the idea that maybe this was His will.

The following morning at our ladies' Bible study, I mentioned my prompting for Thomas's healing. Two other women had been impressed for the exact same thing the night before. Our faith began to soar. We established a prayer chain that would extend through Thursday night and Friday morning, the time of Thomas's surgery. We agreed to pray specifically for Thomas's healing and for a special peace for the five-year-old as well as his family.

Songs of faith and of God's power filled every corner of my life that day. I was exuberant. I was so sure of what God was going to do that I told my neighbor—something I had never had the courage to do before. This time I wasn't afraid to tell anyone, because I knew for sure!

Friday morning was the time set for the doctor to unbandage the finger and do further surgery. I could hardly sleep Thursday night, I was so excited. I envisioned what it would be like: The surgeon would come out shaking his head with a mysterious-looking scowl on his face and say: "I don't understand. His finger is completely healed." Thomas's parents would praise God for this. The doctor and other people in the waiting room would believe in Christ. Our church would rejoice and have increased faith for more miracles. My neighbor would see God's power. And Thomas would have an experience to root him forever in his faith in God. My faith was strong. It was going to be a thrilling day.

Friday morning I decided to join Thomas's parents at the hospital as another step of faith. Thomas wasn't there when I arrived. Maybe they overslept. Finally, they rushed in. While Thomas was getting his bloodwork done, his father relived the last few hours. Thomas had been sick to his stomach and was up most of the night. I remembered our prayer chain and our specific prayer for a restful night. I shrugged off any negative feelings quickly.

The doctor was ready for Thomas in his office. As Thomas and his mother walked toward the office door, Thomas turned to me and smiled a strained smile. I winked at him. Everything was going to be OK. But in a few minutes, his mother returned shaken. The finger had not healed; instead, the entire tip would have to be removed. I snapped up my slipping faith and reminded her that God could still heal Thomas's finger before the surgery.

Thomas went into surgery. We waited and waited. Where was the doctor's puzzled face full of mystery about the miraculous healing? We chatted some more. People from the church stopped by to visit. Other families in the waiting room left one by one after being told surgery was completed. We continued to wait. The ice in the cups melted, and coffee-stained cups sat forsaken on scattered magazines.

Finally, the waiting room door swung open. The doctor smiled as he walked in. He matter-of-factly described the detailed surgery and the good news that he didn't have to remove as much of the finger as he had feared. As much of the finger? What about the total healing? I was stunned.

Continuing the small talk, and pretending to be relieved that the surgery had gone so well, I somehow managed to stay a little longer. We avoided each other's eyes. The echoes of Scripture and words of faith now bounced off the walls with no place to land. As I got into my car, it hit like an iron weight—God had let me down.

The grieving I went through was like the loss of my best friend. To me that's exactly what it was. I had accepted Christ as my Savior at the tender age of five. God had always come first in my life. He had influenced the major decisions of my life—and even the minor ones. I was used to being sensitive to His leading. I had the image of God as a loving Father gently guiding me down life's pathway. I was trying to grow even stronger in my prayer life. I had seen big miracles happen to people who didn't have much faith at all. All I had asked was for God to save a tiny fingertip of a five-year-old boy. Plus, it hadn't been my idea in the first place—but His! Why would my best friend make such a fool out of me?

My mind flipped back to other instances in my life where I had "misinterpreted" God's will. There was the embarrassing time I trusted God to help me sing a solo; and when I got up to sing, I couldn't utter a sound. There was also the time I made a special trip across town, feeling my friend urgently needed me, only to find she wasn't even at home. How could I have been so stupid as to believe God really guided me? However, I couldn't imagine what life would be like without trusting God to guide me. Was I living a farce? I never doubted God was real, but a God who tells you to do something and then lets you fall on your face isn't the kind of God I had imagined. That's when I envisioned Him laughing. It crushed me. I prayed for answers.

The next evening we went to a Christian concert—something I had looked forward to for weeks. I now mechanically went. Tears filled my eyes as I heard them sing songs of faith, trust, and love for their God. How I yearned to feel that way again. But I was so alone now. God had failed me and I hurt so deeply—like death.

I went through the duties of teaching a Sunday School class, saying prayers at bedtime with my children, and pretending to be "fine." Feeling sorry for myself helped a little, but I was miserable. A lump was constantly in my throat, and tears came without much urging. I would make certain my children weren't around, then I would bombard my husband with my unanswered questions about God.

The following week I was listening to a new tape. The words of one of the songs leaped out at me. The message was praising

God—when things went right and when things went wrong. I rewound the tape and listened again. The same message was there, to praise God in every situation. Even for unanswered prayers? Yes, we are to praise God for who He is. That is true praise. I had been so excited about giving God the praise for a miraculously healing. Since God hadn't healed Thomas, I didn't see anything to praise Him about. The song said to praise God *because He is God.*

Another question still hung over me. Why would God allow me to make a fool out of myself by bringing me to a point of saying, "I know this is God's will"? Could I ever trust my knowledge of God's will again? My pastor suggested that perhaps it was actually my pride that was crushed rather than my faith in God. That was a hard pill to swallow. The Bible states that God's ways are past finding out. To believe that I can fully comprehend God's will at all times is placing myself far above the human being that I am. To think I can, or even should, dictate to God a perfect plan for Him to fulfill is also an egotistical idea. I was wrong in my interpretation of God's will. I was wrong because I am human, and that's all right.

Over the days and weeks, the wounds of my broken friendship with God started to slowly heal. I realized He wasn't laughing at me, but instead was using this incident to help me grow, painful as it was. Like the Father I had imagined, He was patiently letting me learn lessons. I talked to other people regarding my disappointment and realized they, too, had similar feelings. Instead of denying my feelings, I looked for answers. I knew I would find them.

Several times since the incident with Thomas, I have felt prompted to pray for something or to do a specific thing. My first reaction is a guarded, "No way. I'm not going to set myself up to be wrong again." That isn't faith in God. That is trying to have faith in myself. There will be times when I don't understand God's will. There will be times when I want something so desperately that I will persuade myself God will work it out my way.

There also will be times that I will fall flat on my face. Preventing these things can't be uppermost in my mind.

Five-year-old Thomas is as happy as ever. His shorter finger goes unnoticed unless you look extra close. If you look extra close you will also see that my faith is stronger because I'm learning that faith is knowing God is in control. I don't need to know what God is going to do or how He is going to do it. Faith is saying, "Thy will be done"—and meaning it!

Jo Edlin is working in the Philippines with her husband, Jim, an Old Testament professor at Asian Pacific Nazarene Seminary. Before leaving, Jo, a registered nurse, taught expectant parent classes. She enjoys her two daughters, Julie, ten, and Janelle, seven. She claims her most enjoyable hobby is being with her friends.

21
My Husband's Brain Surgery

by SUE SCHRADER

December 17, 1980 is a day I'll never forget. Many times since that day I've heard my husband, Alan, say: "I don't understand why this had to happen, but God has a reason for everything."

Alan and I were married on June 15, 1968. We've had a happy marriage and two children: Tina, born May 1969, and Todd, born four years later in April 1973. God has always been a part of our family. We gave our hearts to Him as youngsters and have raised our family for Him.

We have always been active in our church, Memorial Baptist Tabernacle. Alan was ordained as a deacon in February 1980. I teach the kindergarten and first grade class in Sunday School.

In December of 1980, Alan began to have some dizzy spells. He went to our family doctor, who later referred him to a neurologist. On Sunday, December 6, Alan was admitted to Memorial Hospital for some routine tests. By Wednesday the tests confirmed that Alan had a large acoustic neurone brain tumor located behind his right ear. I can remember how the world seemed to close in around us. I guess my first thought was, "This only happens to other people." But now it was right in my own home.

Surgery was set for Thursday, December 17. This meant we would have eight days to wait, more tests, transferring to a larger, better-equipped hospital, and the uncertainty of not knowing. The doctors had given Alan an 85 percent chance of having no malignancy, but they couldn't really say how much damage could occur to the nervous system.

For the next few days I sat by his bedside. At night I would come home to be with the children, then see them off to school the next morning. On the way back to the hospital, I would hardly be able to see to drive as tears filled my eyes. I thought, *My dear husband, only thirty-two years old, and how much pain he is in.*

I felt as though my life was over. I prayed, "Dear God, please help me, I just can't stand this alone." When I arrived at the hospital I would smile so that Alan wouldn't see how upset I was. I never one time let Alan see me cry. I had to be strong for him and for the children. I can truly say that God's grace was and has been sufficient for my every need.

On December 14, Alan was transferred to Erlanger Medical Center. On Thursday, December 17, he would undergo surgery to remove the brain tumor. There was no visible evidence of the tumor.

When we arrived at Erlanger Medical Center, we were taken to the seventh floor Neurosurgery Unit. The hall seemed a mile long. Everything was gaily decorated for Christmas. There were green and white streamers hanging from the ceiling with red bells hanging from the center. My heart sank as I led Alan stumbling down the hall. I kept wishing for the world to stand still. It was eleven days till Christmas, and our children were at their grandparents'. *Why couldn't we be home like other families?* I thought.

The next few days meant more tests and long hours of waiting. The night before the surgery, I remember how Alan prayed to the Lord seeking His will. I must truly say that for me it was hard to say, because I knew all I wanted was for Alan to be all right. I had to realize that the Lord must have His will in our lives.

Alan was a man of strong faith in God. He felt so confidently that everything was in the Master's hands. On the morning of the surgery, Alan was up at 4:00 AM. When I awoke, he was getting ready to take a shower. He was walking around the room with his towel over his arm singing, "It's All Right," a favorite song that our church quartet sings. A portion of the song says, "When my steps are getting slow and it's time for me to go and ole Satan tries to say, it's all in vain; when I cross ole Jordan wide and I view the other side, it'll be all right for the Lord will call my name."

At this point, I could feel chill bumps on my arms, as I looked at a man who could face surgery with such confidence. As 6:30 approached, our pastor, Ronnie Hooker, arrived as well as many family members and friends. Just a little before 7:00, the nurses came to let us know the time had come. Our pastor led one last prayer before Alan was wheeled down to surgery. As I walked down the hall to the elevator with my hand in Alan's hand, my many thoughts were so uncertain. My only hope was in the Lord.

The waiting room seemed so dreary as we waited for the nurses to call and update us at regular intervals. The first time they called, they explained to me that they were beginning the surgery. They said they would call as soon as they could tell me if there was any malignancy. It was around 1:00 PM when the nurse called and told me the tumor was found to be benign. I raised my hand in praise to God as tears began to flow. There were twenty people waiting with me. We all knelt and thanked God for another prayer answered.

The day passed so slowly. Many friends and loved ones came by to visit and to offer a prayer and kind word.

Around 9:00 PM the nurse called to say everything was going fine. I asked her if it was almost over. She told me it would still be several hours, that it was such a large tumor.

When the doctor came down to the waiting room to talk to us, he said this was the largest tumor of its kind that he had ever removed. The surgery had taken seventeen and one-half hours.

The first time I was permitted to see Alan after his surgery was at 4:00 AM on Friday, December 18. I thought I was prepared to see him . . . until the time came. His head was completely shaved, and his whole body was swollen. He was being monitored by several machines. I began to feel as if the doctors hadn't told me everything. *Would Alan ever walk or talk again?* I wondered.

On Christmas Day, the children visited their dad for the first time since his surgery. He could not even hold his head up without support. I remember Todd's words: "I don't believe that was my Daddy." Tina seemed very quiet, but wanted to love and comfort her dad.

For the next eleven days, Alan was in the Intensive Care Unit. The only way he could communicate was with his left eye. He could blink when I asked him a question. His right optic nerve had been damaged, so his right eye was bandaged. Alan's whole left side was completely paralyzed, and the nerves that controlled the facial muscles and tongue had been severed in order to remove the tumor. In the next few weeks, Alan had to learn to talk again. It was so frustrating because he knew what he wanted to say and do, but the brain was unable to send messages to the different parts of his body.

On January 6, thirty-seven days after Alan entered the first hospital, we were going home. I could hardly believe this day had arrived. I felt scared about taking him home. He was still unable to walk, and it was a real struggle just to eat. But with the Lord's help, I knew we could do anything.

We arrived home at 1:30 PM. The children had come home from school early for the big homecoming. We had only been home for about two hours when it began to snow. The children were out of school for six days because of the weather. I felt God had sent the snow just to give our family a few days at home together.

The next weeks would mean I must return to my job at school where I worked as a teacher's aide, and Alan's grandparents would come everyday to take care of him. Every morning I would get Alan up, bathe him, put on his clothes, and get him to the living room sofa where he would sit and relax until I got home. When I came in from school in the afternoons, I would help Alan walk and exercise his arms and legs. In three months, Alan was walking with a quad cane. Every day that Alan took a step, I felt it was a blessing from the Lord. Without the Lord's help, I feel my situation would have been impossible to deal with.

In February we were able to return to church for one service on Sundays. Just being in public with a crowd of people was an emotional trauma. Our friends and relatives were so kind and thoughtful of our feelings. Through their prayers and love offerings, our church was a true source of strength. I feel special gratitude for the love that our parents, grandparents, sisters, brothers-in-law, and other family members and friends have shown us through Alan's illness.

When I look at Alan and our lives, I see a miracle from God. Alan is able to walk. His speech has improved greatly, and the strength in his left hand is still improving. The optic nerve has not yet regenerated itself, but God is still answering our prayers everyday.

I must admit that there were days when my patience seemed to run short, and I wondered if I would ever have a normal life with my family again. But through faith in God our every need has been supplied.

As I write this story, Alan and I have just celebrated our seventeenth wedding anniversary. Our children, Tina, now sixteen, and Todd, twelve, have seen how the Lord has taken care of their dad through many long hard trials and how our family's faith in God has been strengthened. God did not promise everything would be easy, but He did promise He would never leave us.

Sue Schrader and her family live in Rossville, Georgia. She has been a teacher's aide at North Rossville Elementary School for seven years. Sue, Alan, Tina, and Todd are once again active in their church. Sue admits: "Our lives have seen many changes, but now we have returned to a pleasant and happy family life."

22
I Never Got to Hold Her
by PAMELA HADAWAY

"We have an assignment for you," said the voice on the telephone. The call had finally come!

"It's a little girl, born April 10."

After years of infertility treatment and a frustrating experience with our county adoption service, we were parents at last—a daughter to call our own. It didn't matter that she was thousands of miles away in a South Korean orphanage and could not come "home" for several months. She became our baby as soon as we heard the news. Our journey to parenthood had lasted seven years and was full of hopes and heartaches, but now it was over. Our prayers were answered in this little one in another land.

My husband, Kirk, and I had become interested in exploring an international adoption after my mother told us of an agency that placed needy children from other countries—primarily South Korea. I wrote the agency requesting information. When it came we read through the material and then put it aside for a while. I had recently had a second major surgery which we hoped would enable me to become pregnant.

Months passed and the international agency came to mind again. I asked a friend who was hoping to adopt if she had ever considered international adoption.

"No," she replied, "but neighbors of ours recently adopted a baby girl from Korea. I can introduce you to them if you're interested."

We met the family at a neighborhood Fourth of July picnic.

Little Rachel had been in this country only a couple of weeks. She was just over three months old and very sweet natured. Her parents were certainly enthusiastic!

I went over one afternoon to talk to Stephanie, Rachel's mother, about the international adoption process. Rachel's adoption had been arranged by the same agency we had contacted. Stephanie was very helpful and readily answered my questions.

"As wonderful as I thought motherhood would be, it's a thousand times better than I expected." Stephanie's joy was so overwhelming that she could not contain it. It seemed to fill the room.

As I was leaving, she handed me a magazine to read. It contained firsthand accounts of families who had adopted international children.

"It may help you in making your decision," she said.

We read the stories with interest. I was especially drawn to the pictures of the children and their families.

In August we attended a picnic sponsored by an organization of families with international children. We learned that not all of the couples adopted because of infertility problems. Many of the families had biological children as well. They were all eager to share their stories with us.

"You know, what strikes me most about this group is the incredible enthusiasm of the parents," I remarked to Kirk as we drove home.

"Yes, I noticed that, too. None of the usual comments such as 'your life will really change' or 'you can't imagine how different things will be.' "

We heard comments like that frequently and felt they were often said with a note of resignation and given almost as a word of warning. All of that was noticeably absent at the picnic, and it was a refreshing difference. We anticipated changes when we became parents, but those changes were what we longed for most.

The picnic was the turning point for us. After further prayer we decided to go ahead and begin the process. Previously, the idea of parenting an international child had seemed abstract; but when we actually saw the families interacting, we could see ourselves in the role.

We contacted the agency about our decision. The social worker told us, "I will be in Nashville next week. If you can get your completed application to me by then, we can begin your home study right away." After years of waiting, parenthood was just around the corner. All of this time I had thought I was waiting on the Lord, but the thought occurred to me now that perhaps He had been waiting on us!

I wrestled with self-doubts about my ability to parent an international child in the early stages of making our decision. To complicate matters, we had an opportunity to apply through another agency for a local adoption, and their waiting period was much shorter than most other agencies. At this point we weren't sure what to do. We prayed but nothing seemed clear. Sometimes I would think, "Well, let's just go the conventional route. Maybe I'm not up the the special challenges of raising an international child." But the children's faces in the magazine Stephanie had given me haunted me. Even when I tried not to think about it, it was almost as if they were there tugging at my sleeve.

I really wanted a "sign" from the Lord. A friend who counseled me about it finally came out and said, "Pam, the Lord is not going to send you a telegram. You need to clear your mind and see what fills it in the days ahead as you surrender it all to God."

This seemed like good advice, and for the first time I felt a peace about it. I realized I had been mentally arguing with myself, going over the pros and cons and not really giving the Lord a chance to speak to me. In all my turmoil, He couldn't get a word in edgewise.

Deep in my heart, I believe I knew all along that the Lord wanted us to apply for an international child. My faith was not strong and my confidence shaken by fears of the unknown. The melody from the hymn "Trust and Obey" kept coming to mind. A passage in Hebrews jumped out at me:

"So do not throw away your confidence; it will be richly rewarded. You need to persevere so that when you have done the will of God, you will receive what he has promised. For in just a very little while, 'He who is coming will come and will not delay. But my righteous one will live by faith. And if he shrinks back, I will not be pleased with him' " (Heb. 10:35-38, NIV). At the same time the Lord was reassuring me that He would equip me to do whatever He called me to do. I sensed Him telling me that He would really bless us as we followed His leading.

Now the decision was finally made, the papers and forms completed, the interviews behind us. We entered what I think of as the "pregnancy" period—the seven- to nine-month wait for the agency to assign us a child. We discussed names—Nichole for a girl, Brett for a boy. A couple of the mothers in the adoptive support group told me that this wait seemed endless. I thought that after seven years of waiting, seven months would fly by. Instead the days dragged on, and I thought we would never hear the good news that a child had been assigned to us. We told our friends and co-workers about our decision and they shared our anticipation.

When the call came in early June, our excitement was tinged with disappointment when we learned that because of a legal technicality the baby would not be free to leave Korea until she was six months old. That would be in October. We were also disappointed that she was in an orphanage instead of foster care. I had been praying all along that our baby would be placed in a loving foster home, so this caused me some anxiety at first.

We anxiously awaited the pictures and medical information the agency was sending to us. In the meantime we chose her name—Nichole Mee. Her Korean name was Mee Ok Jung. We always referred to her as Nichole, and it was wonderful to be able to pray specifically for her.

I called my neighbor from work every day with the same question.

"Would you mind checking my mailbox to see if the agency letter is there?"

"Of course not," came Karen's quick reply. "I'm so excited I can hardly stand it."

After a couple of days the response we'd been waiting for was shouted into the phone.

"It's here! It's here! Can I open it, please?" Karen begged.

But I wanted to be the first to see Nichole's face—after all, I was her mother. Kirk was out of town so he would have to wait. I dashed home for my lunch hour. The drive never seemed longer. I pulled into our driveway and ran to the mailbox but decided to contain myself and open the thick envelope in the house. This was a special moment for me. It was almost as if Nichole herself was inside the envelope.

Once in the house I forgot my composure and tore into the envelope. The pictures were the first thing to catch my eye. As soon as I saw her, crying in one and looking very sleepy in the other, I rejoiced as though I had just given birth. She became so real to me then. No doubt about it, this was our little girl and I loved her already.

I took her records to a pediatrician as the agency had suggested. As far as I could tell everything looked fine. The doctor would call me with his evaluation as soon as he could.

I found a brass frame just the right size for one of Nichole's pictures and carried it with me in my purse. Since Kirk was still out of town, I called a friend to meet me for dinner and celebrate the occasion. Melody was delighted to "meet" Nichole and even brought a special gift.

The next day was Saturday. Kirk would be returning home that night. In the afternoon, the doctor called with his evaluation of Nichole's medical records. There were reports of two different exams done about a month apart. One was done the day she was born and the other was about four weeks later. The doctor expressed concern that in that time she had gained very little weight —only a few ounces. Everything else looked fine, but his comments about her lack of weight gain made us fearful that she might not be thriving.

This really put me into a tailspin. I got very depressed and immediately gave in to despair, questioning why this was happening. I was angry and upset. The stress of waiting to hear about a baby had taken its toll on me. I had imagined that there would only be good news. I felt so helpless. If only she could come quickly, then I could give her the love and care she desperately needed. I was consumed with a mother's worry.

Something made me mentally step back and look at myself for a moment. I saw an angry, bitter woman and it gave me a jolt. I knew I had two choices: Either give in to despair and disillusionment or put my faith in the Lord, trusting Him to take care of Nichole. I did not like the first option, so I chose to cling to the Lord. By the time I picked Kirk up at the airport that evening I felt much better. Kirk was distressed at the doctor's report but agreed that prayer was the only thing we could do for her.

At church the next morning we introduced Nichole, via her photograph, to members of our Sunday School department and requested their prayers for her. The more we showed her picture to others the better we felt about her situation.

In the following days I immersed myself in the Bible, reading passages that spoke of God's love and care. I recorded many of them in a notebook to be read one after the other as a big dose of assurance. The more I read the more certain I became that Nichole was going to be all right. God loved her more than we did. We could trust her with Him. It was still difficult to think of her in a crowded orphanage. We prayed that one worker would take a special interest in her so that she might feel loved.

I became an obnoxious mother showing her picture to any and everyone. Kirk and I were both impressed by the interest shown in her—even by people who did not know us well. A young woman in a nearby office at work was especially excited about the baby, inquiring daily if we had heard word of her arrival date.

We were expecting to hear an updated medical report as soon

as it came to our social worker from the agency's office in Korea. I was no longer worried about Nichole—just anxious to know when she would be coming to us. A close friend at work always had ears to hear me vocalize my impatience about more waiting. She had also been a great comfort to me in my first anxious moments about the baby's well-being. She was a gifted listener and enabled me to verbalize my feelings.

I began work on the nursery and was getting more excited with every stroke of the paintbrush. I could not resist buying children's books for Nichole. I visualized us reading them together.

In mid-July I took a Wednesday off to tie together some loose ends at home. It had been a productive day. I was in the middle of a project when I heard Kirk's car pull into the garage. I had not expected him for another hour, but did not think too much about it. I was concentrating on my work when I realized he was standing in the door.

"Hi. You're home early," I commented without looking up. I was applying a last coat of paint.

"I heard from the agency today," he said. His voice sounded flat and strange. I looked up from my work and saw the distress in his eyes.

"Why, what's wrong?" I could not imagine what would cause him to act so strangely.

"I don't know how to tell you this, but they are going to have to assign us another baby."

I was stunned. "Why, what has happened?" The thought crossed my mind that perhaps Nichole's birth mother or a relative had come to claim her at the orphanage. Our social worker had told us that this rarely happened, so I had dismissed the possibility. But it came to mind now.

Finally he said, "Pam, she caught pneumonia and died."

Suddenly my world turned upside down. Where? When? What were the details? I wanted to know.

"That is all the information Sue (our worker) gave me. She

called earlier today. I just didn't know how to tell you, so I put off coming home for a while."

I felt as though my heart had burst. My baby was dead! The tears flowed in such a torrent I thought I would never be able to stop them. I thought about her being sick and alone. She never knew she had a "forever" family waiting to welcome her. We never got to hold her. These were my first thoughts.

My tears alarmed Kirk. I just could not stop crying. But even as the tears flowed unchecked, I felt God's unseen arms folding me close to His heart. And I felt no anger toward Him. I tried to tell Kirk not to worry about me; crying was my way of coping.

Kirk called some close friends with the news. I even spoke long distance to a special friend who was vacationing in Florida at the time. I mostly sobbed into the receiver, but she understood. I felt her empathy as strongly as if she were in the room. Another friend came over as soon as she heard the news. She listened and wept with us. She and her husband were expecting to receive word any day about a baby girl they were going to adopt. Someone had contacted our new pastor and he phoned, concerned.

I thought that most people would not understand the depth of our pain, since we had never held Nichole in our arms. We were wrong. Our pastor had requested prayer for us during that evening's Wednesday night service. Afterward the calls came and many of our close friends from church stopped by. One even skipped the service to bring us supper and stayed to share it. Nichole had many friends waiting for her and now they grieved with us. It amazed us that a small unseen baby far away in Korea could touch so many.

The impact she had on our lives cannot be measured. During the weeks I had been praying for her and reading about God's character I began to have a much greater awareness of His love for me. It seemed more real and less abstract. It had always been difficult for me to accept that God's love for me was unconditional. I knew what the Bible said, yet I had difficulty fully accepting His love. As I "claimed" that love and care for Nichole—she became the channel for me to accept it for myself! Even though her death left me heartbroken, I sensed the Lord's tenderness and compassion. I felt no anger toward Him and His comforting arms were there to hold me. I knew Nichole was with Him and free from pain—no longer alone but surrounded by everlasting love. I found a poem, "Faith," by Ella Wheeler Wilcox, that tugged at my heart. I desired to have that kind of total trust because I was beginning to know God as I had never known Him before.

> I will not doubt, though all my ships at sea
> Come drifting home with broken masts and sails;
> I shall believe the Hand which never fails,
> From seeming evil worketh good for me;
> And, though I weep because those sails are battered,
> Still will I cry, while my best hopes lie shattered,
> "I trust in Thee."

Nichole's death made Kirk and me partners in suffering. I realized for the first time that his desire to have a child was as great as mine. Adoption had always been acceptable to him, but sometimes I wondered if he was doing it mostly for me. He was not as verbal in expressing that desire, but I had been mistaken when I thought that meant it wasn't as deeply felt. Nichole's death put those doubts to rest. I had never seen him hurt so much.

A few days after hearing the news we left for New Mexico, where we were scheduled to attend a conference at the Glorieta Conference Center near Santa Fe. Glorieta's majestic setting soothed our hearts and provided a respite from the reminders at home—especially the half-finished nursery. A friend had given me a book on grief, *Tracks of a Fellow Struggler*, by John Claypool. I read it on the plane to New Mexico and found it to be a great source of help in sorting out my feelings and my questions.

Coming home from Glorieta was very depressing. Although I felt God's grace and presence, the pain was still there. I just wanted to go away again and escape from the hurt. Time seemed to creep by at home. I "missed" Nichole as my thoughts had been so full of her. Her picture was burned in our memories.

The agency told us we would be getting another assignment at any time, but we were not yet ready for it at first. We were still grieving for Nichole and one child cannot replace another.

The day finally came when I was ready to hear those words again, "We have an assignment for you!" I had put off finishing the nursery, but now I began to plan again.

When my sorrow was still intense, I had claimed Isaiah 61:3 as a promise for the future. God gave us "beauty for ashes, the oil of joy for mourning, the garment of praise for the spirit of heaviness."

That promise was fulfilled in the second daughter God gave us, Chelsea Elizabeth, who arrived from Korea on October 2, 1985, the day she was three months old.

Our situation has been unique and our crisis unusual. But no one who was close to our situation took it lightly or underestimated the depth of our feelings, and for that I am grateful. I was told that someone at church had made the comment that it shouldn't be too difficult, since we had never even held her. But several women who had suffered miscarriages or stillbirths knew differently and called to express their empathy. A friend who had lost an adopted child to sudden infant death syndrome just a few months after his placement spent hours helping me cope with my feelings and grief. I learned a whole new dimension of the meaning of carrying one another's burdens, whatever they might be.

Pamela Hadaway lives in Franklin, Tennessee. She and her husband, Kirk, delight in Chelsea and each stage of her development. Pamela, a native of Memphis, Tennessee, knows how to be a friend and therefore has many loyal friends. She is a homemaker, a crafts enthusiast, and a sales representative for a Tennessee-based manufacturing company.

Closing

"In peace I will both lie down and sleep;/for thou alone, O Lord, makest me dwell in safety" (Ps. 4:8, RSV).

Late one night, I saw the first streaks of lightning bolt across the sky. Within minutes, great drops of rain beat hard against the windows, and thunder rattled the house.

Not long after, I heard my two-year-old daughter's frightened cries. I hurried to her bedroom and picked her up. "Thunder scare me, Mamma," she cried. Still holding her close in my arms, I laid her on her bed and snuggled close beside her.

"Mamma's here with you now. Are you still afraid, honey?" I asked. "No, Mamma," she said as she wiggled her tiny hand securely in mine and went back to sleep.

As I stayed next to my daughter throughout the long, stormy night, I thought about the dark thunderous nights I, too, had called out with frightened cries to God. It was during those times that I had placed my hand securely in His and had most keenly felt His comforting Presence. He had always brought me peaceful sleep even in the midst of my fears.

I glanced again at the face of my daughter, no longer afraid of the thunder, sleeping quietly. My arms still around her, I whispered a prayer and thanked God for the many times He had picked me up and held me in His strong, loving arms. During the terrifying storms of my life, He had been there close beside me, and I had not been afraid.

Through the stories of these women, you and I have been given a glimpse into their individual crises. They have known how very dark the night can be. Physical suffering, prejudice, misunderstanding, abuse, the death and illness of a loved one, the breaking of a marriage, conflict—both emotional and spiritual—each has coped with hours, days, months, and even years of anxiety and struggle. They have known fear, loneliness, frustration, discouragement, sadness, and grief.

Someone once wrote: "Life is too discouraging, too overwhelming to go it alone." These writers believed that. They did not want to endure their hardships alone. And each, in deep despair, came to realize even more acutely God's comforting Presence. These are the ones who have reached out to God in their despair and have discovered wholeness in Him. Placing their hand securely in His, they have found a peaceful sleep . . . until the morning light.

This is a book of hope. None of us can control our situations ultimately. No doubt, each of us will be faced with our own crises. They may be frightening. They may even seem devastating. But whatever the crisis, you and I, like these women, can find hope in our struggle. For we are not alone. There is One who really does hear us when we call out to Him with frightened cries. Yes! A loving Father watches over us and stands close beside us to offer strength and courage to weather these storms. And, like these women, we can emerge victorious! As our hymnist so aptly writes: [Indeed!] "The night becomes as day, When from the heart we say, May Jesus Christ be praised!"

DENISE GEORGE

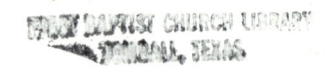